BUILDING
SHOW JUMPS

Show jumping is immense fun.

BUILDING

SHOW JUMPS

Andy Radford

THE CROWOOD PRESS

First published in 2005 by
The Crowood Press Ltd
Ramsbury, Marlborough
Wiltshire SN8 2HR

www.crowood.com

British Library Cataloguing-in-Publication Data
A catalogue record for this book is available from the British
Library.

ISBN 1 86126 792 4

Dedication
This book is dedicated to the memory of Gillian Barlow 1952–2005.
A dear friend who loved her animals and will be sadly missed.

Typeset by Carreg Limited, Ross-on-Wye, Herefordshire

Printed and bound in Great Britain by The Cromwell Press,
Trowbridge

CONTENTS

ACKNOWLEDGEMENTS

I would to thank the following people and organizations for their help in putting this book together: Roger Edwards for helping with the designs and construction of show jumps, Alison Edwards, the riders of the Berwyn and Dee Pony Club, including Abbie Gurnett. I am grateful also to Jamie Radford, Janet Williams, Mary and Gwyn Evans and Paul Gurnett.

A special thank you to Chloe Edwards and Robbie, to Crisiant Radford and Saxon, for allowing me to photograph them using the show jumps.

Unless otherwise stated all diagrams and photographs are the author's copyright.

Show jumps designed and built by the author and Roger Edwards.

INTRODUCTION

Imagine the wind rushing through your hair and the tumult of the horse's hooves thundering beneath your saddle: your mount charges towards a hedgerow, sending the sparrows flying from their perches. The knot in your stomach tightens as fear, excitement and freedom fuse into a sense of the inevitable. Your heart begins to pound in rhythm to the horse's galloping hooves, and the pit in your stomach betrays an element of doubt. The hedgerow, innocent symbol of man's symbiosis with the land, now appears daunting, taller than the steepest buttress on the highest mountain. Then you're there, at the point of no return, resigned to the unknown. And then there is peace, an overwhelming tranquil silence as you find yourself soaring through space like an eagle sailing upon unseen thermals, the ultimate harmony between horse and rider.

Your skyward adventure ceases in an instant as the galloping hooves pound the earth once more. The experience lasted but a second, a mere moment in time – but the memory will linger a lifetime.

Trying your skill, wits and fear in the show-jumping or working hunter arena is probably the ultimate test for horse and jockey. Most riders have ridden their horse or pony over obstacles of varying forms, even if only as part of a Pony Club rally. It's exciting, it's nerve-racking and,

most importantly, it builds confidence: confidence not to just leap the highest pole or rail and come back for more, but an assurance that you can overcome any barrier life throws your way. To totally understand an obstacle is half the battle of conquering it. One factor in understanding a subject is to know how it is built, and comprehending what actually goes into the show jump you enjoy.

This book is a culmination of my experience of construction transformed into a written, step-by-step practical guide. You may be surprised to know that most wooden show jumps are based upon two basic designs. Firstly, there is the standard wing set comprising large uprights, tapering down to small uprights – a sort of triangular affair, if you like. Each upright is connected by horizontal rails and vertical intermediates. Secondly, you have the rectangle-shaped wings with all their uprights the same size. Many interesting entities can be fashioned out of these standard shapes: for example, by joining three more sides to the rectangle you end up with a pillar; and by imposing your own taste in décor you can modify the dull into the sublime. This book deals with these basic concepts, along with instructions and further ideas. However, it is not a step-by-step decorating companion, since this, I feel, is down to personal taste.

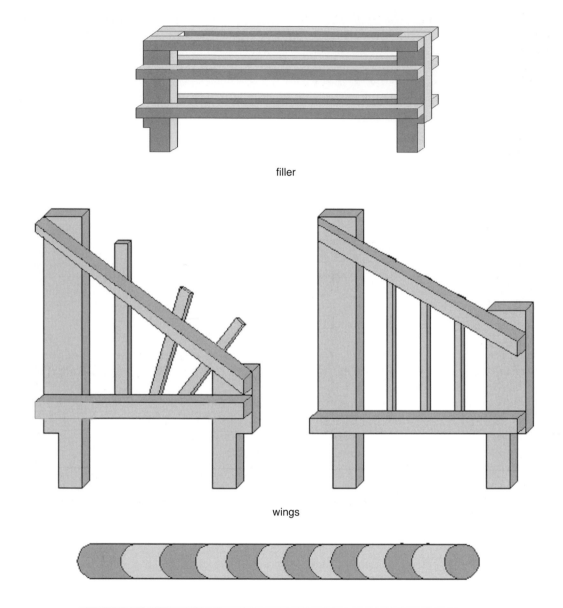

filler

wings

rails and poles

The main parts of a show jump.

The first chapter, 'Getting Started', deals with all the fundamentals of practical work: health and safety, the types of tools needed, and where you can purchase the best materials. Subsequent chapters give ideas and instructions for building your own show jumps. Finally in 'Useful Addresses' you will find a list of the various bodies you can contact if you feel like taking your skills to a higher level, whether on the practical side, or in the exciting world of horse riding.

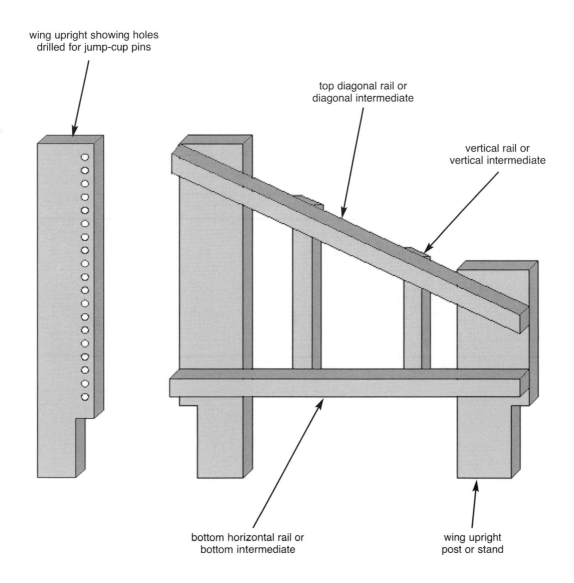

wing upright showing holes
drilled for jump-cup pins

top diagonal rail or
diagonal intermediate

vertical rail or
vertical intermediate

bottom horizontal rail or
bottom intermediate

wing upright
post or stand

The parts of a wing.

CHAPTER 1

GETTING STARTED

Safety

The main factor to consider is the welfare of the animal and the people who intend to use the equipment. At no time should safety be taken lightly, as this could turn out costly in health, finance and time. When erecting any structure, meticulous planning and a diligent approach to the physical work should be common practice, and particularly where horses are concerned, since the smallest of hazards has the potential to cause the largest of problems: for instance, it is very easy to overlook a stray nail lying on the floor or a loose-fitting panel that is about to be blown off by a gust of wind. With the large number of fixings required, even for lightweight tasks, a protruding nail-point or sharp-ended bolt could be easily missed, and these oversights take their toll on ponies, horses, children and adults all too frequently. It is important to realize that horses have an uncanny knack of finding the weak points in any structure, whether it is a set of wings or a free-standing filler, and left unrepaired, these could become an accident waiting to happen.

Tool Safety

Working with hand tools poses the greater risk to the user, although an unattended device will become a hazard to a pony if it is using the paddock you are working in. This is true for all tools. Learning how to use tools in the proper manner can enhance the enjoyment of the work and speed up the job with a minimum of fuss and danger. Electrical power tools make light work of heavy jobs, and some of the projects described later rely on their use. As most of the projects in this book can be performed outside, attention must be paid to the safety advice that comes with the items when purchased. This is all down to common-sense work practices: in damp or wet conditions they must not be used; always use a circuit breaker; uncoil extension cables to their full extent; and make sure they also have an integrated circuit breaker. Electrocution is a serious, sometimes fatal injury, and steps must be taken to avoid this. Check the cables of all power tools for splits on the outer insulating sheaths; needless to say, if the cables are worn, either discard or repair the tool.

Using power tools around horses and ponies is not recommended, and if you must work in the paddock, the animals should be moved to a safe, fenced-off area away from the work site. On no account carry out maintenance work in an enclosed space with an equine: sudden or continuous noise can scare it, cables can be trodden on, and stray screws or nails could cause severe injury. Again, move the animal to a safe area – and preferably not the stable next door, if this can be avoided. When working in a field you should erect a temporary enclosure well away from the work site. This can be done simply with an electric fence. Another major hazard associated with electrical tools is fire. When using drills or power saws in stable blocks the surrounding area must be clear of dry hay and bedding. Adequate fire precautions should be implemented before work commences, and some means to control fire should be in place on all yards as a matter of health and safety.

Hand tools such as saws and screwdrivers are to be treated with respect. It is very easy for the blade to slip and cut through a hand or finger. Believe it or not there is a correct way to hold these tools, called the 'forefinger-thumb' principle, which is more or less the same way as one holds a pen for writing. The forefinger-thumb technique allows the operator to use a tool with the best stability possible. Hammers are another common cause of injury, usually bruised or broken fingers and hands.

Personal Safety

Just as tool safety is a necessary work ethic, personal safety should be regarded equally seriously. Never undertake any practical work without basic health and safety equipment. A first-aid kit (and knowing how to use it correctly, of course) is probably the most important piece of equipment you should carry with you, but basic work clothes such as leather safety gloves and steel toe-capped footwear should be worn at all times.

If you are working in a confined space with a horse, carrying out simple quick routine tasks and there really is no alternative accommodation for the animal, be extremely cautious. Use manual drills and saws instead of electrical ones, and always have an assistant to restrain and soothe the horse, away from the point of work. It would be preferable for the assistant to take the horse out for a walk 'in hand' if possible, instead of keeping it near the work site.

Performing tasks in the open air brings with it further dangers. Heat stroke, hypothermia and fatigue can all catch us unaware. Adequate clothing, high-energy foods, warm or cold drinks (depending on the conditions) and regular breaks should be as essential as the first-aid kit previously mentioned. If the place you are working in is remote, always inform someone of your position and estimated finishing time before you begin your work; that way if something untoward should occur, someone would notice that you have not returned, and will come to your assistance sooner rather than later. The mobile phone has revolutionized safety in the countryside, but some forest or mountain regions have reception blind spots, which could result in your cell phone not working correctly.

Common injuries associated with bad working practices are:

- minor and severe cuts due to misuse of saws, small fencing tools and other sharp-ended items;
- minor and severe splinters from wooden building materials such as fencing rails and stakes;
- impalement from screwdrivers, chisels and crowbars.

Equine Safety

Bad working practice may cause injuries to equine stock. In some cases the damage is devastating, even resulting in the animal having to be destroyed. It is up to the owners or the people working on site (depending on who is carrying out the job) to make sure that the area is kept free from potential hazards. The majority of injuries can be related to bad working practices or absent-mindedness; for instance, a lost nail in the stable or an untrimmed piece of timber could lead to a pricked foot and a hefty vet's bill, with the animal being out of action for a long time. Even something as simple as leaving your lunch box in a prominent place could cause a serious digestive disorder if a horse or pony gained access to its contents.

Equines can also very readily put themselves at risk due to their ingrained 'fight or flight' behaviour if they are startled, and it is important that anyone working in the vicinity of horses understands that they will like as not bolt when startled by a sudden loud noise. Care should therefore be taken to avoid needlessly scaring horses into running blindly around a field, or pulling back suddenly on a tie rope. In the same context it is imperative that other people are warned of when you are about to begin hammering or drilling; thus, it would not be conducive to a good schooling session to have a horse take off across the ménage like a bucking bronco because a contractor picked that precise moment to start banging away at a new course of show jumps. That would certainly compromise relationships with other horse owners! Needless to say, unlike most domesticated pets, equines are more prone to getting into trouble and harming themselves, and extreme care must be taken to protect their welfare.

Purchasing Materials

Choosing the most cost-effective retailer is critical. Unlike other goods, where the price tends to be around the same no matter what shop you look into, the charge for timber produce can vary considerably. Although high street DIY outlets tend to stock small amounts of agricultural hardware, their range of goods is usually limited to a few fencing stakes and rails. Most of their floor space caters for the home and garden market, and as a consequence of this, their timber products tend to be sold at a higher-than-usual price. They do, nonetheless, offer a great range of sundry items such as nails and screws, and can sell you almost any work tool you might need. Where metalwork for equestrian projects is concerned, the only items you might not find in a DIY shop are the jump cups for show jumps.

In a large agricultural suppliers such as a Farmers' Union Co-op store, you will find almost anything you need for the equine market. However, although farmers' co-ops may be able to supply the widest choice of merchandise, it is the dedicated agricultural fencing retailers that still offer value for money when in comes to shopping for basic materials. The prime outlets are sawmills, with their own retail premises: not only can they offer all the timber requirements you will ever possibly need, most of them will supply timber cut to your requirements. And in view of the fact that they cater for the countryside market, you will invariably find an extensive range of sundries stacked on their shelves, probably at the best prices, too.

Working Safely with Tools

Remember that accidents are caused, they don't just happen, and building show jumps requires the use of various hand tools, all with the potential to cause serious harm to the user. Making sure your tools are properly maintained can help produce a safe working environment, and this in turn will make the job of cutting, drilling and chiselling, whilst creating a desired result, more efficient and, in some cases, quicker. Common injuries associated with broken or misused equipment include serious puncture and incised wounds; amputation of extremities such as fingers; eye injury caused by not wearing the correct protection; and electrocution which could lead to death, to name but a few.

Using Powered Hand Tools

Inspect the casing and handle for any cracks and loose fixings. In the case of a power drill, check the auxiliary handles for damage, and make sure they are secured to the tool in the correct manner. Check also power cords for defects such as cracking, fraying, bare wires or other flaws associated with the insulated casing.

The plug should not have faulty or missing prongs, and check that the plastic or rubber casing is held securely with its fixing screw where applicable. Inspect also the plastic cable clamp on the inside; this should be holding the cable firmly in place. Any missing screws here must be replaced, and if a replacement cannot be found, change the plug.

If a power tool is found to be defective, it should be taken out of service and repaired by a qualified technician. Even if you are in hurry to get the job done, the 'temporary' use of a defective unit could have serious consequences.

Make sure, where applicable, that the power tool has the manufacturer's recommended guard, and that this is not loose or damaged. It is important to study the instruction booklet before use. Finally, to protect the operator from electric shock, all power tools should be plugged into a circuit breaker or a low-voltage transformer.

Some Precautions

- Do not use a power tool if you are not sure how to operate it. Enroll on a course at a local college or similar establishment.
- Do not carry the tool around the workshop when it is plugged into an electrical supply, and make sure your finger is not touching the trigger switch. Always make use of the 'safety lock' setting.
- Do not turn the tool on or off by using the plug. Make sure the trigger is disengaged before connecting the power supply.
- Do not disconnect the plug by pulling or jerking the power cord.
- Do not leave an unattended power tool running, and make sure the mechanism has completely stopped before laying it down or disconnecting the plug.
- Do not operate power tools in wet or damp locations, and do not expose them to rain.
- Do not alter cables in order to create a longer connection, as this may lead to

insufficient energy reaching the tool and could also cause electric shock. Only a qualified electrician should attempt repairs to power tools. Always use a proper (undamaged) extension reel, complete with circuit breaker, and make sure it is fully uncoiled. Make sure that cables are free from knots, as this may cause a 'short' or electric shock. Only use extension cords in areas without a power outlet; they should not be used as permanent wiring.

- Do not allow children to play with the tools or their cables, and make sure cords are placed where vehicles cannot run over them. Do not use power tools around children: you will not be able to hear properly over the noise of the power tool, nor will you be able to concentrate on the job whilst trying to supervise a youngster.
- Do not carry power tools by the cable.
- When operating saws and drills, wait until the mechanism has stopped before brushing away sawdust or waste wood.
- Do not wear loose clothing, or gloves when using revolving tools such as drills, and ensure that long hair is tied back.
- Do not use power tools in areas of flammable vapours, and do not clean them with flammable solvents.
- Do not startle an operator, as this could lead to injury. If you are the operator, make sure you warn people before you power up.

Hand Tools

Be careful to use the right tool for the right job; improper substitutes may increase the risk of injury, or damage the item under construction. It is also important to keep tools serviced and in good condition at all times; to this end, wipe metal parts with a rag doused in clean mineral oil after use.

Always check the tool for defects before use, and replace damaged items. All cutting tools should be kept sharp, and when not in use, suitable covers should be placed over blades and saw teeth. Mallet shafts and hammer handles should sit tightly within the tools' heads. Place sharp tools (chisels, saws, marking blades) in the centre of the workbench, making sure that blades or handles are not protruding over the edge of the bench. Store tools in the proper manner after use.

You should always wear appropriate safety clothing in relation to the tool in use: for example, goggles and a face mask for drills and electric saws. Also, the working area must be kept clear of clutter and debris at all times: if the task in hand produces a high quantity of waste, then you should clean and sweep up as often as possible.

If your work area is small and you are using many tools at the same time, wearing a tool belt will come in useful to store equipment. This will save space and ensure the working area is clear from obstruction.

Do not use tools for a job they are not intended to do; for example, refrain from using chisels for levering, and wooden mallets for driving in nails and bolts. Also, try not to use excessive force on tools that are not designed to take strain. Lastly, be careful not to transport sharp tools in pockets other than ones designed for them.

Chisels

There are many styles of wood chisel, each one designed for a specific cutting purpose; you should therefore use the correct chisel for the job in hand in order to avoid inaccurate work. Also, in the interests of good practice you should wear safety goggles or glasses. Other points to bear in mind are these: ensure that wooden-handled tools are free from cracks, splinters and oily substances; and keep the tool sharp at all times by 'honing' the cutting area to the correct angle – blunt tools will make the work difficult, which could result in an untidy, misaligned joint. When you are working, make sure that there are no foreign bodies in the timber such as screws or nails, as these will blunt or damage the blade.

Your body position is important: for instance, when cutting joints or mortises you should maintain a balanced stance, so if the chisel slips you won't fall over. Always make sure that your hands and body are placed behind the cutting edge, and chip timber away from you. Do not strike wood chisels with a metal hammer; always use a wooden or rubber mallet with a wide striking surface.

When finishing a joint or mortise, use only hand pressure to smooth away uneven cuts or burrs.

Always store chisels with their protective cap over the cutting edge.

Hand Saws

As with chisels, use the right saw for the job: a hacksaw, for example, is mainly used for cutting metal. Always check the timber you are cutting for foreign bodies such as nails and screws. And bear in mind that if hand saws are not used correctly the resulting injury could be severe – considering the pressure used when trimming timber, a slip will easily rip bare flesh to the bone.

Always observe the correct method of operation, which is as follows: begin your cut by placing a hand at the side of the pencil guide, making sure that your thumb is pressed against the side of the metal blade. Start the cut with a slow, careful action to prevent the blade from bouncing on the wood; only apply pressure on the 'downward' stroke, as this will ensure that the actual cutting action is maintained away from the body. Clamp timber firmly to prevent it from moving.

It is important always to replace damaged or severely blunt saws, and to keep the saw teeth properly 'set'. Many saws come with a protective plastic cover that fits over the teeth; these are for protecting the tools when stored, and reduce the risk of injury.

After each use wipe the blades (not handles or grips) with a rag doused in clean mineral oil.

Hacksaws

Hacksaws are designed for cutting metal. The blade should be attached with the teeth pointing forwards. Use the entire length of the blade when trimming material, working with steady, firm strokes directed away from the body. The backward stroke should be light to eliminate premature blunting of the teeth.

On long jobs the blade and the material will heat up, so avoid touching these with your hand. To prevent the blade from overheating and snapping, wipe a light oil over the cutting area.

Screwdrivers

Choose the correct screwdriver for the style and size of screw – Phillips' head drivers for Phillips' head screws, Pozidriv for Pozi head screws. Pre-drill pilot holes before joining two sections of timber. This will aid the travel of the screw as well as ensuring that the fixings remain straight and won't veer off at an angle. Pilot holes will also help protect the wood from splitting. Make sure that the drilled hole has a smaller diameter than the screw.

Ensure the screwdriver handle is clean and free from grease and oil; an unexpected 'slip' may result in injury and damaged work. Use a ratchet drive (or Yankee screwdriver) for continuous screw work: this is healthier for the wrists, and results in less fatigue. Other alternatives are powered drivers or tools with a pistol grip. Defective screwdrivers – ones with a bent shaft or a blunt or broken tip – will continually slip off the screw head, damaging work or causing injury. Wooden handles, if split, should be replaced.

Only use a screwdriver for the job it is intended for; these tools are not pribars, levers or chisels. Note that exposing a screwdriver to excessive heat can weaken the metal.

Clamps

Clamps are used for a wide variety of applications; they are very versatile and hold work securely when sawing or chiselling. There are many styles and sizes of this tool available, so choosing the right one for your work-holding requirements is essential. The main points to consider are the size of the timber as compared to the opening (or *reach*) of the clamp, and the depth of the clamp's *'throat'* in relation to the width of the workload. Securing work in a tool that is too small to handle the weight will result in the timber becoming dislodged. At the opposite end of the spectrum, avoid using extra large, heavy clamps just because they have large throats; it is far better to employ a smaller, deep-throated item intended for the size and shape of the timber.

Ensure that the threaded end can turn easily before use. An application of light oil will free movable parts, but avoid contaminating the 'anvil' and 'pressure plate' sections, otherwise the oil may trickle on to the wood. You should also ensure that the pressure plate and anvil come into contact with the work part before tightening; to avoid damage use a thin wooden 'pad' between the anvil and timber. Do not use torque-bars, hammers or wrenches to tighten clamps; most are only designed for hand tension.

Parts of a Show Jump

Show jumps come in many styles, and it is surprising what can be produced using just two basic designs. If you have ever looked at, or ridden over a set of fences, whether in competition or for leisure, you would probably have seen an array of colours, shapes and sizes – and perhaps even wondered if you could build one of these for yourself. In truth, there is no limit to what can be produced with a little imagination, skill and a regard for safety. The following chapters will guide you through the construction of various interesting show jumps, complete with ideas and designs for poles and fillers. I have always found, when writing this style of book, that it pays to begin with the very basics, then lead the potential builder on to the more complicated techniques – the methods that actually put the projects together. To understand and know the various parts of a construction is always a good place to begin.

The largest sections of a show jump are called *wings* or *stands*; these can be anything from simple barrels to ornately profiled supports. With a few exceptions (explained later), wings sit on independent feet (the reason for this type of foot is explained in Chapter 2). Drilled into the main uprights of a wing is a series of holes for the *jump-cup pins*: these enable the height of the fence to be raised and lowered, depending on the experience of the rider and horse. Jump cups are made of galvanized metal or plastic, and hold the show jump's *rails* and *poles*. The plastic variety is the safest form of cup, as metal fittings tend to have sharp edges and corners.

Another method of holding poles is to screw metal or plastic factory-made strips on to the wings' uprights: these are useful

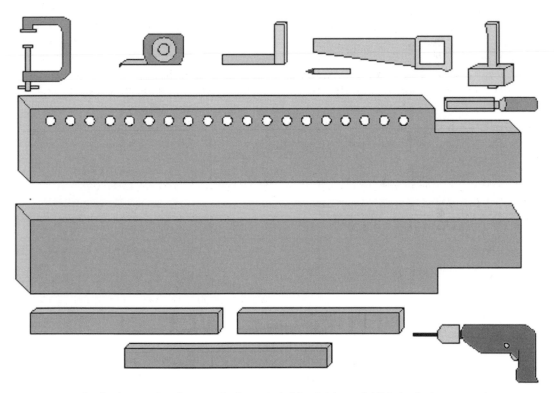

saw all rails down to the sizes required, create halving joints, and drill holes for jump-cup pins

The stages of construction and the tools required.

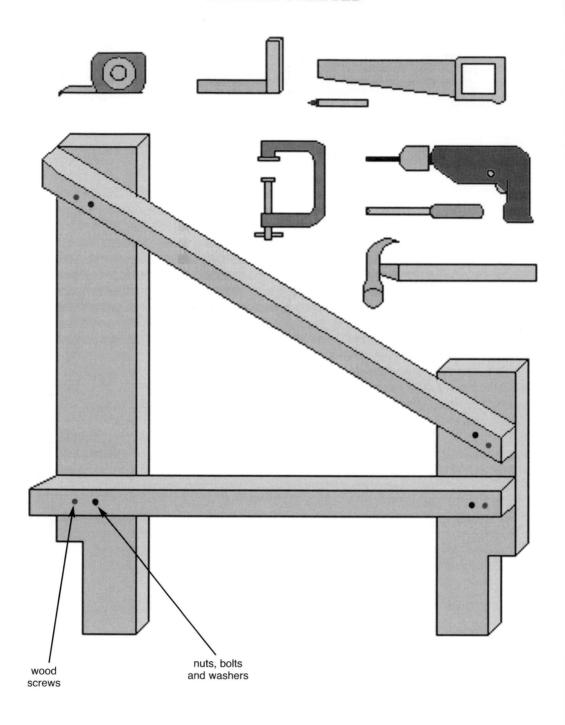

wood
screws

nuts, bolts
and washers

Stage 3 of wing construction.

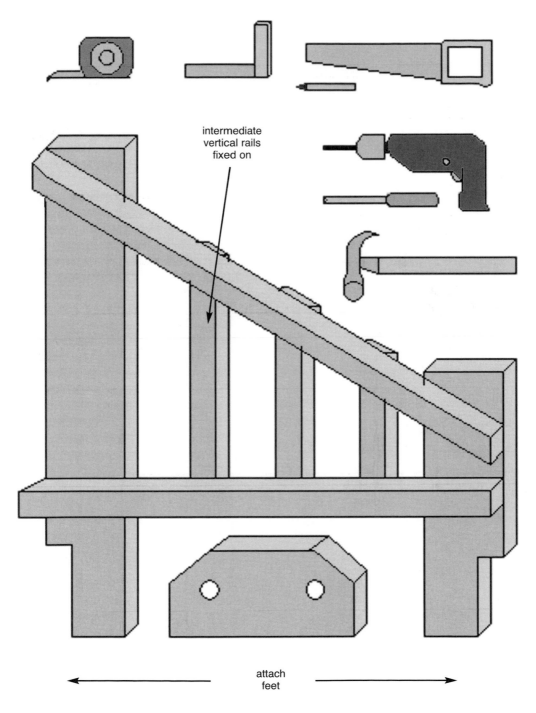

intermediate
vertical rails
fixed on

attach
feet

Stage 4 of wing construction.

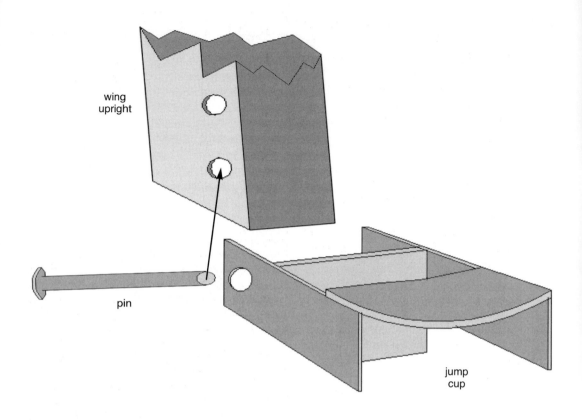

wing
upright

pin

jump
cup

A jump cup showing the method of attachment.

because of their preformed holes, allowing them to hold safe plastic jump cups.
Another advantage is that they immedi-
ately do away with the painstaking task
of having to accurately measure and drill
the wings for pins. This type of cup is
designed to break apart under specific
strains, ensuring less risk of a fall to
horse and rider. From April 2005, the
British Show Jumping Association
(BSJA) has ruled that this type of safety
jump cup is to be compulsory for supporting the back and centre poles on spread
fences. Spread fences are obstacles that
have a width element as well as a height

element; they usually consist of two or
three sets of wings.

Fillers, rails and poles can also be
made in numerous shapes, sizes and
colours. As a rule they are designed to
match the wings they sit between, but
there is no hard and fast law concerning
this. They come in different types, and
include the standard pole, a plank with
end pieces designed for resting on cups,
and more complicated elements such as a
gate, and also brush sections – these are
just the common ones. With a little imagination more fascinating obstacles can be
assembled such as free-standing, mock

brick walls that fit in between wings designed to look like stone pillars, or brush fillers that sit between standard wings. There is no limit to what you can accomplish, provided health and safety are given priority at all times.

We have discussed the basic parts of a set of wings, but since this book is concerned with their construction, a more in-depth look into the various constructional sections is essential. Part names will be described throughout the following chapters, and to save the need to repeat everything for each jump, please continually refer back to the following description. The sections of a wing are:

- front or main upright (the large timber that holds the jump cups);
- back upright (the rear support);
- top rail (connected horizontally or diagonally between the main and back uprights);
- bottom rail (connected horizontally between the base of the main and back uprights, leaving enough room to connect the feet);
- intermediates (this is timber that is affixed vertically or horizontally between the main and back uprights);
- feet (these are obvious);
- back plate (the metal or wooden plate used to hold the feet against the front and back uprights).

Making a Template for Jump-Cup Pins

As discussed, poles and rails rest on cups that are attached to the wings, and a series of holes to accommodate these must be drilled into the wing uprights. Measuring and drilling these holes is a time-consuming task, especially if you decide to build more than one show jump. It is therefore easier and quicker to make yourself a template for the purpose of marking the pin holes on the upright: this means that you will only have to measure once.

All that is required is a length of 5ft × 4in (1.5m × 10cm) timber. An old offcut of tongue-and-groove board or similar material will be ideal. Most wing uprights contain around fourteen 0.5in (12mm) holes, with their centres evenly spaced at 3in (7.5cm) intervals. Initially measure 1.5in (3.7cm) from the edge of the template, and mark this measurement at regular intervals down the length of the template to give a uniform line of holes. With a long straight-edge aligned against these marks, scribe a pencil line from top to bottom. Using the tape again, and working from bottom to top, draw a mark every 3in along this line: these will be the centres for the drill holes. With a 12mm augur or twist drill bit, inserted in an electrical drill or manual brace, drill out the fourteen holes. Chapter 4 shows one of these templates in action.

CHAPTER 2

CREATING STURDY FEET

With the exception of the box jump, all of the wings described in this book use the same style of foot and an identical method of attachment. As a result this chapter is relevant to most of the constructions, and should be referred back to regularly. Some wings, however, will require joints of different width; this will be explained in their sections.

Show-jump feet are perhaps the most important element where strength and safety are concerned, and they should be designed to keep a set of wings safely erect without splintering if subjected to

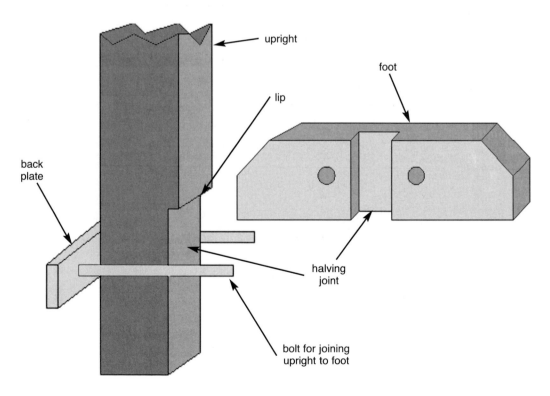

Parts of the feet.

force and pressure. It is for this reason that they have to remain independent from the main construction, and connected directly to a wing's upright using screws or nuts and bolts. The preferred method is to use metal back plates along with the appropriate fixings (explained later).

The only method by which a foot should be affixed to a wing is by a 'halving joint' to eliminate lateral and vertical movement. Although this is not an essential safety concern, it does, however, reduce the occasions one has to readjust the jump, which in turn could result in premature wear and tear. Another good reason for using 'independent' feet is storage or transportation: it is easier to stack show-jump wings on a trailer or in a storeroom when their feet have been removed, This will also mean the risk of serious damage is kept to a minimum.

Material and Tool Requirements

- 2 × 2ft (0.6m) × 6in (15cm) × 2in (5cm) wooden planks (these planks often come in 10ft (6m) lengths and would be suitable for constructing five show-jump feet)
- Tape measure
- Tri-square
- Pencil
- Wooden or rubber mallet
- 1in chisel (this is a minimum size)
- PVA wood glue

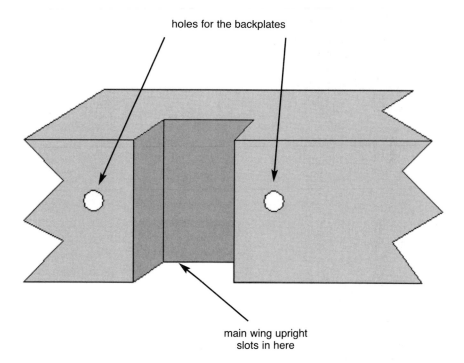

holes for the backplates

main wing upright
slots in here

Halving joint for the feet.

Measuring the 2ft section of foot.

- Hand drill or electric drill
- Wood drill bit suitable for the size of fittings used
- 2 × metal or wooden back plates
- Spanner or socket suitable for the size of fittings used
- 1 × 39in (1m) length of 25mm threaded rod (or whatever size is available)
- 8 × nuts and washers (size will depend on the diameter of the threaded rod)
- Sturdy workbench with vices or clamps

(Note – the second part of this section refers to the uprights, and the material requirements for these are given in all of the wing chapters. For reference purposes the statistics of the uprights are 4in (10cm) × 2in (5cm) × height required for the jump type.)

Method of Construction

If you have purchased 10ft lengths of timber for the feet they will need to be sawn into equal 2ft sections. You will only require four of these sections for one set of wings, but if you are making a full set of jumps it is best to cut the full quantity at the same time and put them aside for

Using a tri-square and pencil to mark the saw guideline.

later use. Please note that feet are not required for free-standing wings such as boxes or pillars.

Place the length of timber on a strong workbench, or lay it flat on level ground. With the tape measure and pencil, draw a mark at every 2ft interval. Next, at each 2ft mark, draw a straight pencil line down the 6in face; this will highlight the areas to be sawn. Re-check the measurements before proceeding. Making sure that the timber is firmly clamped, cut through the pencil lines with a hand saw. To create an accurate joint channel, these initial cuts must be straight and vertical.

There are two easy methods for creating a straight saw line: the first, and probably the most accurate, is to use a carpenter's tri-square; the second is to utilize the straight edge of a hand saw.

Now the first set of feet has been cut to size, the next consideration is to smooth down all sharp corners and edges of the wood. Although there are some commercially constructed wings with rectangular, acute-edged feet, sawing these areas away adds to the overall safety and aesthetics of the show jump. Just two simple, angled saw cuts on each corner can add security and elegance to an otherwise

Carefully sawing the foot section.

bland part of the show jump, whilst reducing risks. Furthermore consider this fact, if a horse were to stumble on his approach to the jump, or as he took off or landed, contact with a sharp-cornered foot could cause severe injury to the rider or animal.

To make these two small saw cuts, place the timber on a solid work surface, preferably a workbench. Choose which horizontal edge is going to be the top (the opposite side to the area that actually touches the ground), and measure between 6–8in (15–20cm) from the end, towards the centre. Mark this spot with a pencil, and do the same from the other side. From each end, measure 2in (5cm) towards the bottom of the foot, and again, mark this with a pencil. Using a straight edge such as a ruler or tri-square, draw a pencil line from the 2in mark to the 6in mark, creating an angled guide. Repeat this on the opposite side. Making sure the timber is firmly clamped, saw through these angled lines as accurately as possible, thereby cutting away the sharp corners. Using an electric sander, surform rasp, wood file or sandpaper, smooth away all edges and corners until they are rounded.

Working out the centre of the foot for the joint channel.

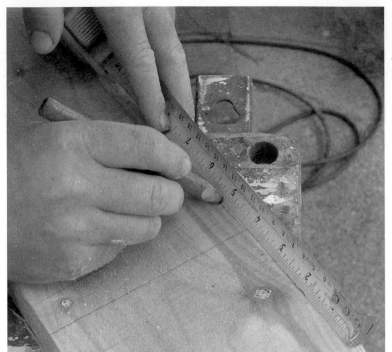

Measuring 1in either side of the foot's centre mark to create the saw guidelines for the joint channel.

Marking the guidelines for the aesthetic angled cut.

Measuring the depth line for the joint channel. This can be between 0.5–1in.

The next phase is to cut away a section of the foot so that the main wing upright can slot in tightly. Depending on the style of wing under construction, this joint, called a 'halving joint', will vary in width. The majority of uprights, however, will use the same measurement. The only set of wings, described in this book, which will require slightly wider joints are the ones for the 'spread jump' (explained in Chapter 6).

The halving joint should be created on the centre of the foot, and the most accurate method of finding the centre is to run the tape measure down the length of the 2ft (60cm) timber and place a pencil mark at 12in (30cm). The front edge of the main wing upright is 2in (5cm), so this means

that the joint must be cut to accommodate it. With this in mind, measure and place two pencil marks, 1in (2.5cm) either side of the previously scribed centre. Place a tri-square against the 1in marks, and draw two straight lines (or saw guides) down the 6in (15cm) face of the timber; check that these lines are 2in apart. The depth of the halving joint should be at least 0.5in (1.25cm). With a ruler or tape measure, mark this measurement by scribing four individual lines on the top and bottom edges of the foot, which in effect will be an extension of the saw guides. Again, with a ruler, join these lines together. The latter has helped establish a depth gauge for the saw.

Drawing the depth with a straight edge.

Carefully sawing down the joint's guide lines.

Using a chisel to cut the joint channel.

Cleaning and smoothing the base of the joint channel.

An alternative method of creating joints is to safely use a power tool.

To make the task of chiselling out an accurate joint easier, a saw should be used to cut through the guide lines: to achieve the best result, it pays to be diligent and precise with the sawing action. Working the tool whilst all the time keeping a strict eye on the guide and depth lines, will produce the desired outcome. A third cut can be made down the centre of the channel to further aid the clearing of the waste wood. There are two points to bear in mind during this stage: firstly, make sure you saw down the inside of the guide lines; we don't want to fashion channels too large for the main wing uprights – it is better to make them slightly smaller than required, as this will guarantee a good, tight fit. The second point is the depth: ideally the saw should reach the depth lines on both edges at the same time, so there is no risk

of the joint's becoming uneven: to this end, make sure the saw is level.

The next job is to chisel out the waste wood from the joint.

The second part of the halving joint is the 'cut out' on the main wing uprights. Before continuing, mark an end of each upright to signify the base. Next, turn the wood so that its 2in side is facing upwards, and then clamp it securely to the workbench. Remembering that the height of the feet is 6in, measure this amount from the bottom end of the upright, and mark it on the 2in face. With the tri-square and pencil, draw a straight line through this mark, from one side of the face to the other. Re-check your measurement, and ensure the pencil line is exactly 6in from the timber end. Using a ruler, draw a 1in (2.5cm) line down both 4in (10cm) faces. This will be

Marking the upright for the foot's joint.

Highlighting the depth of the foot's joint.

Sawing the foot guideline to a depth of 0.5–1in.

Using the chisel to cut out the joint for the foot on the upright.

The finished joint.

Connecting the foot by slotting the upright into the joint channel. Note how the lip rests on top of the foot section; this stops the upright from slipping down.

Securing the foot to the upright using the metal back plate.

A good tight fit.

a continuation of the first line. Repeat this on the timber end, and place a mark on both 4in faces. Now, scribe straight lines from the bottom markers to the end of the 1in lines. What you should be looking at now are two 6in lines, one on each side of the timber, exactly 1in from the upright's edge. These are the cutting guides.

The next phase is to cut away the section within the guides. Working on the 2in timber side, place the saw so that the teeth are exactly over the pencil line: keeping the saw horizontal and linear, cut through the line until the teeth reach the 1in depth markers on both sides of the upright. Next, working from the bottom of the timber, saw through the guides

that connect the 1in markers. For this particular task it may be easier to use a jigsaw or, if one is available, a bench saw. With careful cutting by hand it is possible to achieve a good result. If you don't want to use a saw, the waste wood can be cut away by using a mallet and chisel but the result may be uneven.

The next job is to drill the feet so that the bolts can be inserted in order to help secure them to the wings. If you are using pre-drilled, steel back plates, they should be placed in a central position on each foot and used as a template for the drill holes. With a pencil, draw around the inside of the back plates' holes, then mark the centres ready for drilling. Depending

Marking the foot for the bolts' pilot holes. Making use of the metal back plate will ensure accurate spacing.

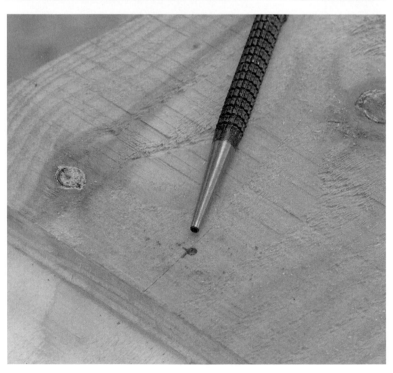

The guide mark for drilling.

Drilling the pilot hole.

Using a brace and bit to drill pilot holes.

on the diameter of the bolt – ours were 10mm – a matching or slightly wider twist drill bit should be used for drilling into the feet.

You can now check if the uprights and feet fit correctly. Start by pushing the bolts through the front of the feet, then slot the joint channel over the upright, making sure that the lip rests on the top edge of the foot. Next, push the back plate over the bolts and add washers and nuts.

Turn the nuts initially by hand until they begin to tighten, then lock them with a spanner or socket until the back plates clamp both uprights.

If steel back plates cannot be found, then you could create your own with the rail off-cuts. The principle of securing them to the feet is the same. They can, however, be high maintenance, and will not last as long as their steel counterparts.

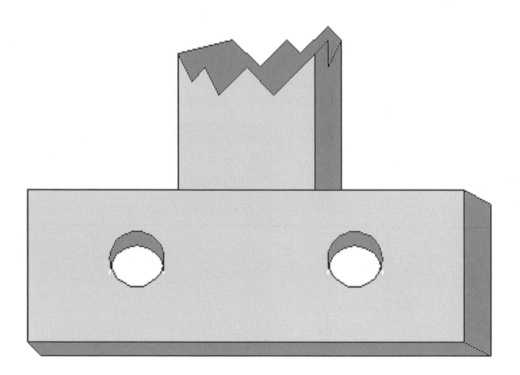

You can use wooden back plates made out of rail offcuts.

CHAPTER 3

BUILDING A BASIC FANTAIL WING

Most riders at some point in their lives will jump competitively, even if it is just in a 'clear round' ring. Having the opportunity to practise at home will enhance their performance at competitions, and of course is vital during the early training of both horse and rider.

A show jump consists of two stands, usually called wings, an arrangement of poles that are supported by the wings, and possibly a filler. A filler is generally used in conjunction with poles – the pole(s) on top, dictating the height of the fence, and the filler literally filling the space beneath the pole(s). Fillers can consist of boards, brush, or a fake brick wall: there is a whole range of possibilities, and owning just one pair of wings can offer the rider many interesting scenarios, depending on the filler used. Obviously owning a whole set of fences will increase the range of challenges, as the rider can then learn to negotiate doubles and turns, and build up his skills to practise over full courses.

Safety is of paramount importance to both pony and rider, and an incorrectly assembled obstacle has the potential to seriously injure equines and humans. Wings must therefore be constructed with a high centre of gravity so they fall easily out of the way when pushed; and

poles and rails must sit in relatively shallow, preferably factory-made jump cups so they, too, fall away easily and do not risk entangling horse or rider. Every inch of the filler and wings must be 'equine friendly', with no sharp edges and no protruding metal bolts. Generally the feet of the wings should be detachable, but this is more of a construction issue than a safety requirement, because most stress and wear occurs around the lower section. Permanent, fixed feet will eventually break off, sometimes beyond repair.

The project described in this chapter is for a 4ft-high (1.8m) set of wings. To minimize their weight, both wings taper down to a height of 2.5ft (76cm). The overall length of each wing is 3ft 3in (1m), with the intermediate rails fixed in 'fan' fashion to give the finished obstacle an ornate look.

Material Requirements

(Please note that the sizes of timber given relate to the vital statistics of the book's project show jump. Most sizes of timber are sold in standard lengths, and may have to be purchased as such.)

- 3 × 10ft × 4in × 2in (3m × 10cm × 5cm)

square rail (for the jump's front and back uprights)

- 3 × 12ft × 3in × 1in (3.6m × 7cm × 2.5cm) square rail (for the jump's frame construction)
- 1 × 8ft × 6in × 2in (2.4m × 15cm × 5cm) section of plank (for the jump's feet)
- Nuts, bolts and washers (for connecting intermediates to uprights)
- 1.5in (38mm) screws (for constructing wings)
- 4 × metal, pre-drilled back plates (used to help attach the feet). If these are hard to come by, another method is described later in the chapter.

Tool Requirements

- Electric or rechargeable drill
- Rechargeable screwdriver or drill
- Hammer or rubber mallet
- Spanners or socket set
- Tape measure
- Hacksaw or grinder
- Hand saw
- A file suitable for smoothing metal; a grinder can be used in its place
- Surform rasp or sander for smoothing sharp edges

Construction

Cutting and Fitting

Firstly, make the feet as described in Chapter 2. Ideally the show jump should be constructed in a workshop, using a firm work surface, but acceptable results can be achieved outside on hard, level ground. The first job is to separate the timbers. The 10ft × 4in rail is going to be used for the jump's main supports; this is

The 4ft and 2ft timbers with bottom, horizontal intermediate.

the section that holds the jump cups. The 3in × 1in rail is for the back supports, and the 12ft × 3in × 1in rails are for the intermediate braces, the part of the jump that gives it shape and appearance.

Begin by sawing the 10ft × 4in rail into two equal 4ft lengths, and place them to one side. Next, make two 2.5ft (76cm) timbers from the remaining 10ft × 4in × 2in timber, and store them next to the main supports. Take one of the 12ft × 3in × 1in rails, and measure and cut it into two 3ft (90cm) timbers.

Before continuing, cut the foot joints on all four uprights as described in Chapter 2. Take one of the 4ft supports and one 2.5ft back support, then measure 8–10in (20–25cm) from their bottoms (the bottom of the supports is where the show jump touches the ground, and so will not be seen when the feet are joined. If your sawing was not accurate, it is a good idea

to use these rough cuts at the base, not for constructional reasons but merely for looks). Working from the bottom of the uprights, measure 6in (15cm) towards the top. Mark this measurement using a tri-square or other accurate guide; ensure the measurements are the same on both timbers. Taking one of the 3ft rails, lay it parallel to the marks, making sure both ends are flush with the outside edges of the uprights. This bottom rail will eventually be bolted to the show jump, but as a temporary holding method it should be screwed in place; one screw at each end will suffice.

Assembling the Basic Frame

Working just above the rail, establish the distance between both uprights, then,

Checking the width of the uprights with the tape measure.

The diagonal intermediate has now been sawn to size.

using this measurement as a guide, adjust the top of the back upright against the main front one. The two uprights should be exactly parallel, and it is important not to disturb this gap because doing so could upset the balance and look of the finished wing; the best way to ensure that the correct distance is maintained is to clamp the rails on, minimizing any movement. Using the remaining 6ft section of rail, carefully place it on the frame, ensuring an overlap on either side of the wing. Before screwing this rail into place, recheck the measurement between the front and back timbers, and adjust if needed.

The wing is now rigid enough to be moved. The next step is to drill a hole through each corner of the wing: these are for the nuts and bolts that hold the frame together. The drill holes must be as close to the centre of the uprights as possible to avoid splitting and future weak-

ness; drilling completely through timber can cause unsightly splitting when the bit pierces the other side. You can avoid this, to a certain degree, by laying the timber on some old rail and allowing the bit to cut into this on its journey through. Before inserting bolts, recheck the gap between the two uprights, and adjust if required.

With the wing still in position on the ground, gently drive the four bolts through the holes using a hammer. Be careful, at this point, not to push them all the way, especially if you are working on a hard surface such as concrete: doing so could spoil the threads, making it difficult to screw nuts on later. When the bolts are inserted, stand the wing up, holding it firmly whilst gently driving them home. Finally the washers and nuts can be attached, then tightened with a spanner or suitably sized socket.

Drilling pilot holes for the wood screws.

Drilling pilot holes for bolts.

Gently tapping bolts home with a hammer.

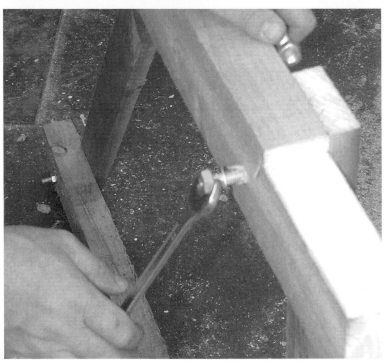

Tightening the nuts with a wrench.

Attaching the vertical intermediates. Note how the rail overhangs the diagonal. This will make it easy to create an accurate saw cut for the top of the fantail.

Securing the vertical intermediates with nuts, bolts and washers.

The finished fantail wings with some undercoat painted on.

The fantail jump painted and ready for action.

Now that the basic frame has been constructed, the intermediate rails can be affixed. We built the project jump wing for this book using three intermediate rails on each wing, one attached more or less vertically and the other two offset at a slight angle to give the obstacle the interesting, fan-like appearance. How one places these rails is a matter of choice, but the gaps between each timber should be less than 4in (10cm) and no wider than 8in (20cm), otherwise you risk trapping a horse or pony's hoof should it stand on the wing. Each timber should be affixed with four screws, using two at each end after pre-drilling to avoid splitting the rail. Before attaching the feet, any overhanging timber should be sawn flush with the jump. Make and attach the feet according to the instructions in Chapter 2.

The fantail jump in action.

CHAPTER 4

RECTANGLE WINGS

Although very elementary in design, rectangular wings can add variety and a touch of professionalism to a set of show jumps. Unlike the fantail jump wing (described in Chapter 3), simply changing the arrangement of the intermediate rails can produce a surprising variety of effects; and you don't even have to use rails to produce an interesting pattern – adding a section of plyboard can introduce a range of décor possibilities. Rectangular wings look excellent with a full complement of fillers and poles, and with fillers carefully chosen to match the wings both look good, and are a pleasure to use as well.

The following project describes the construction of one of these sets, using external plyboard instead of intermediate rails. Attaching board has many aesthetic advantages, since you can decorate it in any style of motif or sponsor's advertising that takes your fancy: the possibilities are endless. You could even make a couple of sets of rectangle-boarded jumps: the shape may be the same, but if one is decorated differently from the other, they will stand out as individual. This design is attractive for its simple shape and appearance, yet it has the potential to look more complex, especially when richly adorned in personal decorative design.

There are two ways to put these wings together. An advanced method requires the creation of joints that allow the top and bottom horizontals to fit flush inside the main wing uprights. If you don't feel confident with that, the same technique used for the fantail wings (described in chapter 3) will fulfil the task adequately, but the finished article might look somewhat unprofessional.

Material Requirements

- 4 × 5ft (1.5m) × 4in (10cm) × 2in (5cm) uprights (these will probably have to be cut from two 12ft/3.6m rails)
- 4 × 2ft (60cm) × 3in (7.5cm) × 1in (2.5cm) rails (make these out of one 12ft timber rail)
- 2 × 2ft × 6in × 2in boards (60cm × 15cm × 5cm) for the feet
- 2 × 4ft × 2ft (1.2m × 60cm) external plyboard panel
- PVA wood adhesive
- 8 sets of suitably sized nuts, bolts and washers. The bolts should be at least 2.5in (63mm) in length if using joints, or 3.5in if you are attaching the top and bottom horizontals using the standard method
- 2 × metal back plates predrilled for the feet (wooden back plates can be fashioned out of small pieces of rail)
- 4 sets of suitably sized nuts, bolts and washers (for connecting the feet)

- A selection of 1.5in (38mm) wood-screws for connecting the panels and horizontal rails

Tool Requirements

- A stable work area (workbench or level area of ground)
- 2 × clamps
- Tape measure
- Tri-square
- Hand saw or electric saw

- Hand drill or electric drill with bits matching the diameter of the bolts and jump-cup pins. Where the jump cups are concerned, it is advisable to use a slightly larger diameter bit than the pin, as it allows the jump cup to be removed and inserted without being forced
- Wooden mallet
- 1.5in wood chisel
- Screwdriver suitable for the heads of the screws you are using
- Marking pencil

Measuring the 4in × 2in timber for the uprights.

Method of Construction

Cutting and Sawing

The first stage of the project is to saw all the timber to the correct size, and make the feet and upright joints as described in Chapter 2. Using a firm, secure and level work area, begin by taking one 12ft × 4in × 2in rail and secure it to the work area. Using a tape measure from one end of the rail, place a mark at 5ft (1.5m) with the pencil. To achieve an accurate measure-ment, ensure that the tape is positioned parallel with the upright's edge. With the tri-square, draw a vertical saw line down the 4in-width side of timber. Carefully saw through the vertical line, ensuring that the workpiece is clamped and cannot move when forced by hand, and the tim-ber is clear from anything that may obstruct the saw. The section of wood being cut should remain clear of the workbench: as such it is good practice to support the opposite timber end. You can do this by resting the wood on a prop,

Sawing the 4in × 2in timber to create the uprights.

leaving ample space under the saw line. Be aware that the saw could snag as you work towards the end of the cut, as the wood begins to close around the blade.

An easier method is to enlist the help of an assistant who can hold the timber end for you and adjust the position of the wood as and when required. If you just allow the work to fall when you reach the end of the cut, you run the risk of splitting the upright. To continue, measure a further 5ft distance from the end of the newly sawn timber, mark with the tri-square, and cut to size. Repeat this for the second 12ft timber.

With the uprights cut to size, the next job is to create the second part of the halving joints for the feet (described in Chapter 2), and the joints for the four horizontals that hold the wings together.

Now the joints on the uprights for the top and bottom intermediates must be fashioned. These should be deep enough to take the whole 1in thickness of the rail in order to create a flush face for the ply-board, which will be affixed as the last

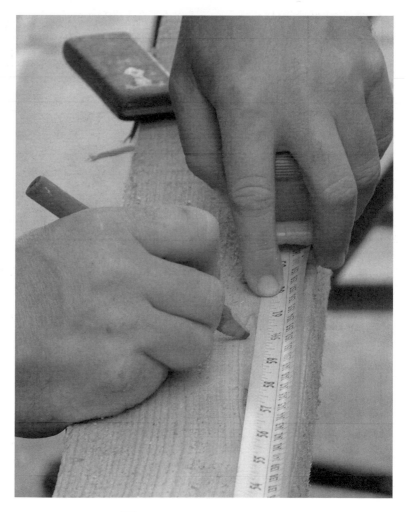

Measuring the upright for the joint channels.

*Marking the joint
channel guidelines with
a tri-square and pencil.*

*The two saw guidelines
have now been marked.
They should be 3in
apart.*

Marking the joint channel at the bottom of the upright. Again, the two lines must be 3in apart.

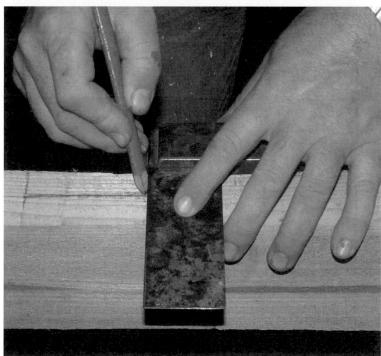

Creating the depth line for the joint channels.

Sawing down the joint channel guidelines.

Chiselling out the waste wood for the joint channel.

The finished channel. You can also use this to help with aligning the other joints required for the wings.

part of the project. The plyboard itself has a maximum length of 4ft (1.2m), which means that the distance between top and bottom joints has to be precise. An inaccurate channel could result in an insecure attachment of the board, with screws missing the timber behind.

A further consideration is the aesthetic balance of the wings; as such the plyboard has to be positioned correctly in relation to the joints. This can only be achieved if the joints' guidelines have been accurately measured.

Assembling

Begin by sorting the main uprights into two pairs. The best way to do this is to lay them out on the ground against each other. Unlike the majority of show jumps described in this book, where each pair of wings is a mirror image, the constructions discussed here are identical. The reason for this is that the timbers on all the main uprights are the same height, therefore it really does not matter on which side you create the joints, as the wings can be turned around to form a pair.

Assuming that the second parts of the halving joints are already made, take two uprights and lay them side by side, and make sure that the cut-outs for the feet are both at the same end. Now turn one upright until both cut-outs face towards the outside (facing away from each other). Place an identifying mark on these timbers to indicate that they are a 'pair': this can be anything you choose, but ensure the same symbol appears on both workpieces. Repeat this for the second pair of uprights, and keep these uprights in pairs at all times.

Measuring from the bottom of one pair of uprights, place a pencil mark at 9in (22.5cm) and a further mark at 12in (30cm). With the tri-square, draw two straight guidelines across the timber's 4in face, one through the 9in (23cm) mark and another through the 12in mark. You should now be left with two parallel lines 3in (7.5cm) apart, along the width of the each upright. Next, scribe 1in depth guides on the 2in-width sides of the

All the wing parts are now ready to be joined together.

Applying a layer of PVA adhesive to the joints.

Using a mallet to gently force the intermediate into the joint channel. Note how the end of the rail is flush with the outside edge of the upright.

Attaching the intermediate to the upright using power screwdriver.

Attaching the intermediate to the upright manually.

The completed rectangle frames.

workpieces: these are the cutting guides for the bottom joint.

The next guides will be for the top horizontal timbers, but the measurement here will be slightly less overall. Measuring from the top of the uprights, place a pencil mark at 3in (7.5cm), and a further mark at 6in (15cm), and use the tri-square to draw the guidelines across the timber's 4in face. Again, these parallel lines should be 3in apart. You will also need to pencil in depth guides as described earlier. Before chiselling out the joints it is advisable to recheck the measurements we have just discussed to ensure that the lines closest to the top of the uprights are exactly 4ft (1.2m) apart from those at the very bottom. It is now time to cut the joints using the same technique described in Chapter 2 for the feet.

The next exercise is to slot in the 2ft × 3in × 1in horizontal timbers that were sawn to size at the beginning of the project. To start, lay each pair of uprights on

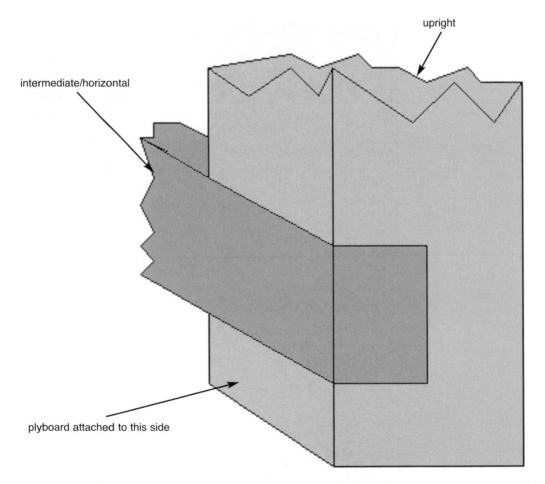

upright

intermediate/horizontal

plyboard attached to this side

The joint for the rectangle wing.

a firm, level surface and make sure that the joints for the feet are facing away from each other. Next, take one 2ft horizontal timber and test it in each of the joints. You may feel a slight resistance as the wood is pushed down: this is fine. If it is obvious that the channel is too narrow, rather than saw a large chunk off the upright, which runs the risk of forming an excessively wide joint, trim it away in small stages until the horizontal can be positioned with little or no restriction.

Working on one joint at a time, smear some PVA glue around the base of the channels. Next, slot in a 2ft horizontal, making sure that its end is flush with the outside edge of the upright. Repeat this on the upright's second channel. You may have to gently coerce the wood with a wooden mallet; if this is the case, use a block of waste timber between the tool and the timber. With the two horizontals now secured in the first upright, bring the second upright in line with their opposite

Measuring for a 2ft plyboard panel.

ends. Again, ensure they are flush with the outside edge before pushing them home. Lastly, drive in four screws, somewhere near the outside corners of each joint, through the horizontals and into the uprights. To avoid splitting the intermediate, drill pilot holes first. Take a note of the position of the screws, as you will need to make allowances for the bolts that will eventually shore up both wings. Repeat the same procedure for the second set of uprights.

Attaching the Boards

As the screws are now holding the joints together, you can connect the boards whilst the PVA glue is drying. If you have purchased an 8ft × 4ft (2.4m × 1.2m) sheet of external plyboard it will have to be measured and sawn to size. Ideally you should carry this out with the workpiece clamped to a secure bench, on a surface area large enough to brace the bulk of the board. If you don't own, or do not have

Sawing the plyboard using a length of baton as a cutting guide.

access to a suitable bench, most large retailers will trim the timber to the size you require, but they may charge for the service.

Assuming you have purchased 8ft × 4ft ply and are cutting your own panels, lay the board flat on the workbench, with at least 2ft hanging over the end. This will set it up for the first cut. Measuring from this overhang, measure 2ft down one of the 8ft edges on the ply, and draw a mark with the pencil. Extend the tape to 4ft (1.2m), and scribe another pencil mark. Repeat this procedure down the opposite, 8ft edge of the ply so that all four marks are opposite each other. Next, with a long straight edge, join both 2ft marks with a pencil, then do the same to the 4ft marks. These represent the outside edges of the ply when affixed to the wings. It is important, then, to recheck that both lines are parallel and correctly distanced apart.

Sawing through board of this size and thickness can prove quite tricky, especially when using a hand saw. A number of problems can arise, including veering off the guidelines, the saw becoming trapped, and the overhanging section continually flapping about in time with your cutting motion; the latter is very annoying whilst you are trying to concentrate on a perfect straight cut, and can lead to mistakes or, at worst, could damage the veneer of the ply. Enlisting the help of an assistant would be advantageous as they will be able to support the overhang, leaving you free to carefully work the saw down the guideline.

The easiest tool to use is an electric jigsaw, as it is quick and very efficient when cutting straight lines. Some people are able to saw freehand with this tool; unfortunately most of us aren't that accurate. The problem can be solved by clamping on a cutting guide across the panel's width, taking account of the extra distance due to the saw's base plate. All you have to do now, apart from ensuring you have enough cable on the saw to finish the cut and it is kept clear from the blade, is to apply a small amount of pressure against the guide whilst working down the panel. After the first panel has been cut, unclamp the remaining section and move it so that the second cutting line is clear of the workbench. Saw the panel as just described.

You may find that the edge of the veneer on the underside of the sawn plyboard is slightly damaged due to the strokes of the jigsaw. You can purchase a blade for this material that is designed to minimize the problem. If the damage is light, there is no sense in throwing the workpiece away, just rub the edges down with sandpaper and apply some wood preservative into the spoiled areas. Most of the damage can be hidden if you fix this side to the wing uprights.

The sawn boards are placed on the uprights, directly over the horizontal timbers. If all your measurements have been correct, the panels should be flush with the outer edges of the intermediate timbers. Before drilling pilot holes for the screws, clamp the plyboard to the wings. Drill a minimum of eight evenly spaced pilot holes through the panels, down the length of both uprights, and a minimum of four evenly spaced holes into each horizontal timber. It is then just a matter of driving the screws home.

The next job is to drill out the holes for the four corner bolts. Choose a drill bit matching the diameter of the fixings, and then place some waste wood under the wing to avoid damaging the work when the drill bit penetrates the other side. Be careful to avoid the fixing screws used earlier to secure the joints. Lightly tap the bolts through with a hammer, then place a washer and nut over the threaded ends. Tighten the nuts home with the correct size spanner or socket.

Whilst the wings are still lying flat, use the jump-cup template (explained in Chapter 1, 'Getting Started') to highlight the positions of the jump-cup pin holes. Place some waste timber under the uprights, then drill these holes using a bit slightly larger in diameter to the jump-cup pin. To achieve a perfect hole, make sure the drill is held as straight as possible.

Earlier we discussed how to craft the first half of the joints on the feet. It is now time to attach them to the wing uprights, which involves a simple process of just slotting the timber into the previously chiselled-out channels. To finish, push the back-plate bolts through the holes drilled on the feet, place the back plates,

Marking the holes for jump-cup pins with the aid of the template.

*Drilling the
holes for
the jump-
cup pins.*

*Drilling the
holes for
the fixing
bolts.*

Gently tapping in a fixing bolt with the hammer.

washers and nuts over the threaded ends, then tighten with a spanner or suitably sized socket. The very last job, before decorating the wings to your own taste, is to smooth away any sharp splinters and protruding fixings.

Variations of the Rectangle Wing

The boarded rectangle wing is one of my personal favourites, but it isn't the only entity that can be created with this style of framework. Replacing the plyboard with two or three vertical intermediate timbers can produce a very attractive picket-fence style. Even if you decide to use boards, there is nothing to stop you sawing out shapes such as flowers or trees with the remaining ply, which could then be fixed to the panels to form raised sculptures. To build the picket-fence wings you will need the same materials (minus the plyboard, of course) plus an extra 12ft length of 3in × 1in timber

Cutting away sharp ends and protrusions.

The completed rectangle wing set.

The rectangle wings decorated and ready for action.

(you should already have a 4ft section remaining after cutting the horizontal timber).

Method of Construction

Build the basic rectangular structures as described earlier in the chapter, but instead of sawing the plyboard, measure and cut the 12ft × 3in × 1in timber into three equal lengths of 4ft. This now makes a total of four intermediates, two for each wing. Next, space them out equally on the top and bottom horizontals, ensuring they are parallel with the uprights. Remember you need to leave sufficient room between the rails to allow the safe passage of a horse's hoof should it accidentally trample the wing.

Another, more aesthetic option is to purchase enough wood to bring the intermediates level with the top of the uprights. This will entail measuring the intermediates to a length of 4ft 3in (130cm). Altogether you will need just two lengths of 12ft × 3in × 1in rail, but you will be left with a little extra at the end of the job. To add a refined touch,

why not round off the tops to give the wings an elegant appearance?

Perhaps the best advantage of owning this style of show jump, panelled or otherwise, is the enhancement that can be gained by standing three wings together to form two types of obstacle side by side. All you need to do is drill jump-cup pin-holes on all of the uprights, as opposed to just two.

Ideas For Fillers

For best results, wings and fillers ought to be coordinated in style and colour, although there is no hard and fast rule governing their set-up. The panelled wings, for example, would look better if you were to hang matching planks from their jump cups. You can create a symbiotic effect by hanging a collection of complementary poles along with one board on the obstacle. The picket-style rectangles would look good, with a large gate filler or a narrow gate affair hanging below a selection of colour-coordinated poles.

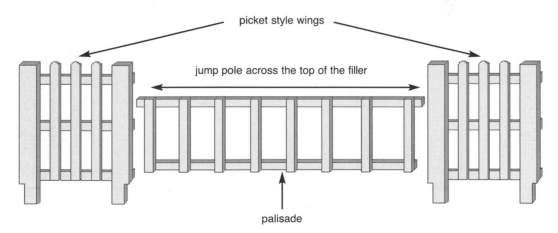

A rectangle jump variation showing picket-style wings and palisade filler.

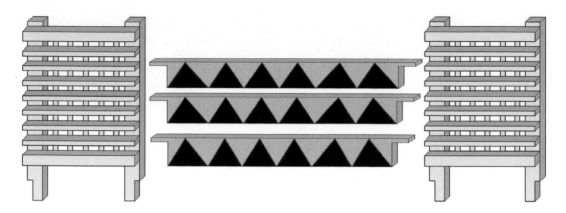

An alternative style to the rectangle panel wings.

Board Filler

Next to the conventional show-jump pole the board filler, or plank, is just as basic and easy to create; the only work involved is to establish a means for it to sit on the jump cups. You can purchase factory-made brackets that affix to both ends of the board, which means you won't have to saw the timber in any way, leaving you free to indulge your imagination with a paint brush or set of exquisitely shaped transfers. The least expensive option involves a minimal exercise with a saw to actually fashion DIY hangers yourself.

Material Requirements

- 1 × 8ft (2.4m) × 6in (15cm) × 1in (2.5cm) treated wooden board

Tool Requirements for DIY hanger

(You will only need a screwdriver and perhaps a drill for pilot holes if you have purchased factory-made hangers.)
- Hand saw or jigsaw
- Tape measure
- Tri-square
- Pencil
- Sandpaper or electric sander

Method of Construction

Working on a firm surface, preferably a workbench, secure the board with clamps to prevent unwanted movement. With a tape measure, scribe a mark 2in (5cm) down the 6in edge from one corner. Working from the same corner, but con-

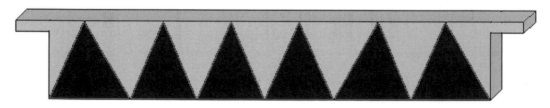

A board filler

centrating on the 8ft edge, scribe another mark, this time at 3in (7.5cm). Using the tri-square, draw a straight guideline from the 3in marker, down the whole 6in face of the board. Next, position the tri-square in line with the 2in marker, then draw a second line until it joins first guide. Repeat this on the opposite end. You should now be looking at two 3in × 2in rectangles at each corner of the board. Shade these in or draw a mark to remind yourself not to cut through these sections, for they will eventually be the hangers.

With the saw, carefully cut through each line up to the point where the two guidelines meet. If the waste wood does not fall away, gently coerce it with you fingers. Lastly, smooth down all sharp corners with sandpaper or an electric sander. The board can now be hung on jump cups, but if you require a stronger finish the hangers can be enclosed with thin metal strips.

Gate Filler

This filler, I feel, suits rustic wings more than it does decorated ones, as the obstacle is supposed to represent the type of gate you might see around agricultural or equine establishments. However, that

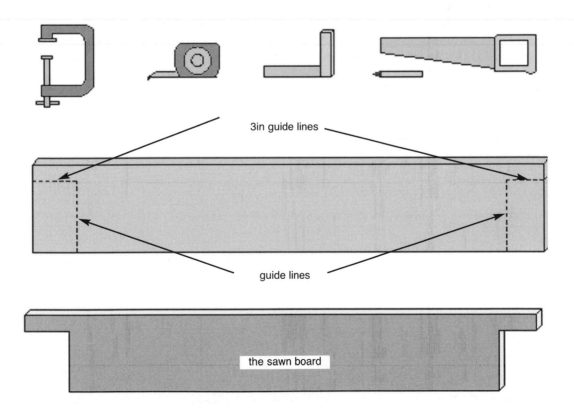

Creating the hangers for the board filler.

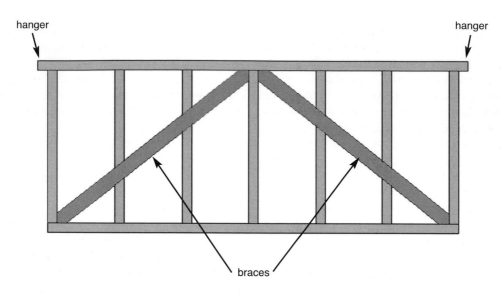

A gate filler

doesn't mean to say that it won't look appealing if daubed in whatever pattern you choose. The most important factor is constructing it to a high enough standard so it will withstand continual use. The gate filler always looks good on a show-jumping course, adding a challenge and variety.

Material Requirements

- 41ft 6in of 3in × 1in treated timber rail; though you may need to buy four 12ft rails. In case you find a retail outlet that will saw the timber for you, for the physical statistics of the filler you will actually need:
- 1 × 8ft 6in (2.6m) × 3in (7.5cm) × 1in (2.5cm) rail (the extra 6in will be used as the hangers)
- 1 × 8ft (2.4m) × 3in (7.5cm) × 1in (2.5cm) rail
- 5 × 3ft (90cm) × 3in (7.5cm) × 1in (2.5cm) rails (these are for the gate's vertical intermediates)
- 2 × 5ft (1.5m) × 3in (7.5cm) × 1in (2.5cm) rails (used as braces to strengthen the gate)
- 8 suitably sized nuts, bolts and washers
- A selection of 1.5in wood screws

Tool Requirements

- Electric drill with suitable bits for the diameter of the bolts and for pilot holes
- Screwdriver
- Hammer for gently tapping the bolts home
- Suitably sized wrench, or socket for the nuts
- Hand saw
- Tri-square
- Pencil
- Tape measure

Method of Construction

Working on a firm and level surface, such as a paved or concreted area of ground, take one of the 12ft rails and lay it down. Extend the tape measure 8ft 6in from one of the ends, and then place a mark on the wood. Using the tri-square and pencil, draw a straight line through this mark, down the rail's 3in face. Supporting the workpiece firmly (ideally with a clamp), carefully saw through the guideline until the section is trimmed. This timber is the top horizontal of the gate. Before placing to one side, draw a mark 3in in from one end and highlight it with a bold, straight line down the width of the timber. Repeat this for the opposite end. The guidelines here represent the outer edges of the gate, whilst the 3in sections represent the hangers for the jump cups. While you are working with this rail you might as well saw off the 6in on the remaining length to make the first 3ft intermediate.

The next job is to measure and saw the bottom horizontal to a maximum length of 8ft, and then store it with the top section until you are ready to put the frame together. With the top and bottom horizontals out of the way for the time being, concentrate on the remaining intermediate pieces. Using the techniques previously described, measure and saw one 12ft rail into four equal 3ft lengths, then store them with the first intermediate, the one made at the beginning of the project. This just leaves the two 5ft braces, which can be sawn off one rail. Again, measure and cut as before.

The timbers are now ready to form the gate filler. Firstly, lay the larger of the two horizontal sections down on the work area (the rail with the extra 6in for the hangers). Take the second horizontal and space it roughly 3ft apart from the first; for the time being, this timber will act as support for the vertical sections when fixing them to the top rail. Next, lay a 3ft intermediate against the inside of one of the bold guidelines on the hanger rail and align it parallel, making sure the edge is just touching the line. After drilling a pilot hole, drive in one wood screw to join the two together. It is important that the screw is not driven through the centre, as this is set aside for the main fixing bolt (explained later). Use the same method to affix the intermediate on the opposite end of the hanger rail.

Concentrating now on the lower rail, adjust it until both ends are in line with the edges of the two intermediates. This action is likely to misalign the vertical timbers, so you may need to adjust these until they are parallel with the bold guidelines on the top and bottom rail. When you are satisfied, attach them with wood screws. The basic framework has now been put together, but before continuing you should make sure that it is exact and not crooked. The best method is to measure both diagonals from top right to bottom left, and top left to bottom right corners: if the two measurements are identical, the frame is 'true'.

Attaching the Remaining Intermediates

To achieve a balanced result, the remaining three intermediates must be evenly spaced apart. This will require measuring the area between the inside of the two end rails, which in this case actually comes to 90in (228cm): it is from this figure that the centres of the last three rails are equated. These are 30in (76cm) respectively. Next, the area between each intermediate should be found. Knowing that the centre of each vertical is 30in and the timbers themselves are 3in wide, we can subtract that figure to end up with a total of 20.25in (approx 51cm). If the last equation is transferred on to a length of spare rail, you can produce a 'spacer' to help in placing the verticals.

Using the spacer, lay it along the length of the top horizontal then push its end against the inside edge of an end rail. Next, abut one of the remaining intermediates to the opposite end of the spacer and screw the timber down. Move the spacer to the bottom horizontal, and repeat. Continue down the length of the frame, affixing the last verticals in the same manner.

The very last sections to work on are the two braces. Before you start, the gate frame should be carefully turned upside down and placed firmly back on the work area. Working from the central intermediate, take the first 5ft brace and angle it down towards one of the bottom corners. You will find that the brace rests on both horizontals. You now need to make a couple of angled cuts so the brace is able to

sit tightly between the centre and end verticals. Adjust the brace until its lower edge passes through the inside corner of the middle intermediate and its upper edge bisects the inside corner of the end vertical. Clamp the brace into position. Concentrating on the top centre again, draw a pencil mark on both of the brace's edges to highlight where it comes into contact with the inside of the vertical. Join these marks with a straight pencil line. Repeat this at the bottom inside corner. Once you saw through these lines, the brace should settle nicely between the uprights.

The final job is bolstering the gate filler with nuts and bolts. Turn the frame upside down so the braces are touching the work area, and place waste wood under each drilling region. Pilot holes should be drilled through all four corners and through the top and bottom parts of the central intermediate rail. Bore a fur-

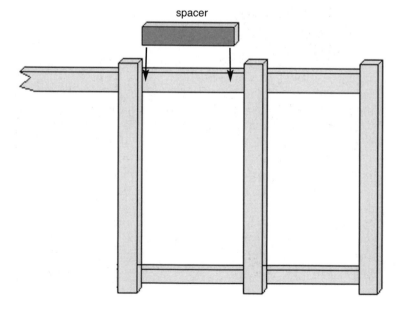

Using a spacer to help achieve accuracy when connecting the gate's intermediate rails.

ther bolt hole in each brace, where they cross the second and third vertical. Insert the bolts and lock them down with washers and nuts. Lastly, smooth away all sharp areas and protruding screw points.

Narrow Gate Filler or Palisade

The construction of this filler (8ft (2.4m) × 2ft (60cm)) more or less follows the method detailed for its larger cousin. Fewer materials will be required because there is no need to add braces and (stating the obvious) the vertical intermedi-ates are shorter. Refer to the following materials list, and construct this project by repeating the procedures of the larger filler.

Material Requirements

- 3 × 12ft (3.6m) × 3in (7.5cm) × 1in (2.5cm) treated rail
- 6 sets of nuts, bolts and washers
- A selection of wood screws

Tool Requirements

Please refer to the construction of the large gate filler.

A rectangle jump in action.

CHAPTER 5

STANDARD TALL WING

The standard tall wing is the most common style around. It is the basic design you will see at amateur show-jumping events, consisting of a large upright on the front and a smaller one at the back, with three, sometimes four vertical intermediates. The one drawback with this mainstay of the jumping world is the weight: these wings are heavy. Nevertheless, a personal collection of jumps would seem incomplete without a couple of these wings standing proud on the course. The following project describes the construction of a set of rustic wings, with the fillers that complement this design described towards the end of the chapter.

Material Requirements

- 2 × 12ft (3.6m) × 4in (10cm) × 2in (5cm) treated timber (for the four uprights)
- 2 × 12ft (3.6m) × 3in (7.5cm) × 1in (2.5cm) treated rail (for the bottom horizontal and the diagonal pieces)
- 2 × 12ft (3.6m) × 2in (5cm) × 2in (5cm) treated rail (for the wings' intermediate verticals)
- 4 × 2ft (0.6m) × 6in (15cm) × 2in (5cm) boards (for the feet)
- 4 suitably sized nuts, washers and bolts
- A selection of wood screws

- Non-toxic wood preservative or dye

Tool Requirements

- Electric drill with suitable bits for the diameter of the bolts and for pilot holes
- Screwdriver
- Hammer
- Suitably sized wrench or socket for the nuts
- Hand saw
- Tri-square
- Pencil
- Tape measure

Method of Construction

Create the feet and joints on the uprights as described in Chapter 2. Take one of the 12ft × 4in × 2in timbers and secure it firmly to the work area. Extend the tape measure down the length of the timber and mark off 2ft (60cm) on the 4in face with a pencil. Leaving the measure in place, draw a mark at the 4ft (1.2m) and 9ft (2.7m) points. Using the tri-square, scribe a straight line through each mark to make three sawing guides. Next, carefully saw through the guides, using the tool as accurately as possible. This makes two short uprights and the first tall one. Take the second 12ft × 4in × 2in rail and

Stage 4 of wing construction.

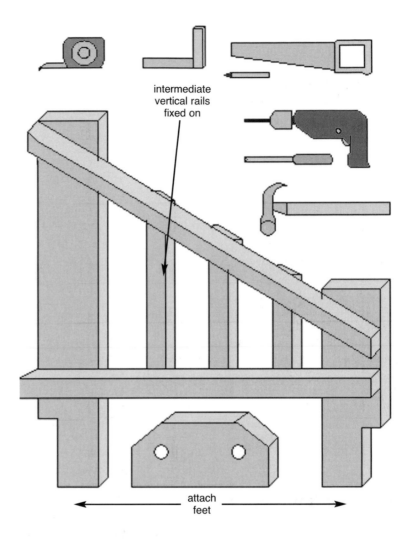

intermediate vertical rails fixed on

attach feet

measure 5ft (1.5m) down its length, then saw it to size.

After moving the uprights to one side, take the first 12ft × 3in × 1in rail, and secure it to the work area. With the tape measure and pencil, measure and mark two 3ft (90cm) points (6ft in total), and then make two more sawing guides using the tri-square and pencil. Carefully cut to size, and write a reminder on the pieces to indicate that these are the bottom horizontals.

Much of the saw work involved from now on requires diagonal cutting through the face of the timbers. You could work out these angles on paper, then transfer them to the wood; in principle this is fine. In practice this method rarely works, because wood is a natural substance, and no matter how straight a procured section of rail seems, there will always be an element of warping. You may find, after you have painstakingly sawn your angles, that the top diagonals and intermediates will not fit flush with the edges of the wings as desired. Really, the most effective measure is to physically align your timbers to the frames. This will be explained in more detail a little later. For now, measure and mark the top diagonal sections at 5ft, then saw them accordingly. The actual finished length of these will be 4ft 6in when trimmed, but you will need this extra for marking.

The intermediate sections can be measured and affixed when the wing frames have been joined together. Needless to say, that is what we are going to do next. To begin, measure and mark 9in (22.5cm) from the bottom of one tall upright, and do the same with one of the shorter uprights. With the tri-square and pencil, scribe a straight line across the 4in face, ensuring it bisects the previous marks. Next, lay both uprights on a level area of ground and position them so that the feet's halving joints are facing towards the outside. When you have done this, spread the timbers until they are roughly 3ft apart and parallel. Take one of the 3ft bottom horizontals, and place its bottom edge against the top of the guideline on any of the two uprights. Adjust the rail until the end is flush with the upright's outside edge, then drive in one screw. Now align the horizontal to the second upright in exactly the same fashion, and join with one wood screw. The area between the two uprights must remain equal throughout the course of construction, so use the tape measure to inspect this distance as and when you feel necessary. As a temporary brace, lightly tack on a spare length of rail, spanning the uprights, a short distance above the horizontal. Avoiding the holding screws, drill a bolt hole through both ends of the horizontal and into the upright, ensuring that you have placed waste wood under the drilling areas, between the ground and workpiece. Then insert the bolts, and secure them with the nuts and washers.

The following phase deals with sawing and connecting the top diagonal. To help achieve an accurate, angled cut, the outer edges of both uprights can be used to define the pencil guidelines. Working near the top, push the diagonal underneath both uprights. With the temporary brace crossing the frame, the wing is stable enough to sustain some movement without becoming misaligned. Next, adjust the diagonal rail until its top edge bisects the outside corner of the tall upright whilst crossing the inside corner of the short upright at the same time. Using the outside edge on the shorter upright as a template, draw a straight pencil guideline down the entire 3in width of the diagonal. Repeat this procedure on the opposite end of the diagonal rail. The timber is now ready for sawing.

Place the diagonal back on the wing, but this time it must go on the same side as the bottom horizontal. Adjust the workpiece until both ends are flush with the outside of the uprights, then secure with nuts, bolts and washers. Before moving on to the vertical sections, clamp the jump-cup template to the 5ft upright, and mark and drill the holes for the pins (you will not have to do this if you are using jump-cup strips).

The wing is now ready to take the vertical, intermediate rails, evenly spaced apart. The best method of doing this is to make a spacer representative of the distance between each vertical rail. The actual centres of the verticals come to just over 9in, which means if a spacer of 4.75in (12cm) is used, the vertical intermediates will be equidistant.

The technique for cutting the intermediates is very similar to the one we have just used on the top diagonal. Firstly, turn the wing upside down, because these timbers should be fixed on the opposite side from the horizontal rail. To begin, measure, mark and saw six pieces of 2in × 2in rail in 4ft (1.2m) lengths, and store three on one side. Next, lay the spacer on the bottom horizontal and abut it tightly against an upright. Taking a length of the sawn 2in × 2in rail, place this against the free end of the spacer. Before drilling the screw's pilot hole, ensure that the vertical timber is flush with the bottom edge of the horizontal intermediate. You should have noticed by now that the wood extends beyond the wing's frame at the top – this is supposed to happen.

To continue, move the spacer and lay it on the top rail. Again, butt it to the upright. Now adjust the intermediate until it is tight against the spacer's opposite end, and then screw it to the frame.

Use this system for the remaining two timbers. Before attaching the feet, add one more screw to each end of the intermediate rails. The last job is to trim down the vertical rail by using the top rail as a guide for the saw.

The first wing is now complete bar painting on the wood preservative. To construct the second wing, follow the instructions just described – though before you go ahead, remember that in the second wing the timbers are affixed on the opposite side from the one you have just built, so you must first be sure to place all the rails on the correct side. Do this by standing up the finished wing, then look at the frame from the front edge (in front of the tall upright), and make a note of where all the affixed timbers are: the horizontal rail and their corresponding diagonals is the outer side of the wing, whereas the vertical sections will be on the inside. So now take a new 5ft upright, and stand it against the one on

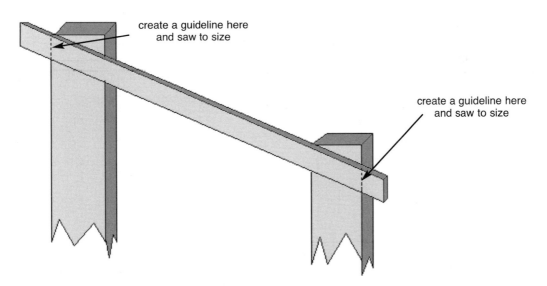

create a guideline here
and saw to size

create a guideline here
and saw to size

Sawing the diagonal intermediate.

the finished article, on the inside – the side of the vertical 2in × 2in rails. On the open, 4in face of the new timber write 'diagonal and horizontal rail', or scribe some other symbol to remind yourself where these rails should go.

To construct the second wing, follow the steps we have just discussed.

Fillers

Any style of filler can be used with these wings, but because this project is 'rustic' in character, the first filler that comes to mind is the 'brush'. The brush jump represents a hedgerow, and for me it conjures up images of horses and riders galloping through field and meadow, leaping from one boundary to the next, an idyllic portrait of olden days, like the ones depicted in oil paintings. A brush jump

adds this sense of charm to any course, and also helps to soften the stark uniformity of the other man-made obstacles.

A brush filler can become quite heavy due to the amount of constructional material it contains, and because of this it should be constructed as two smaller identical structures, instead of one relatively large and heavy object. It is not much fun dragging a cumbersome, bulky 8ft frame around a jumping course, and you should bear this mind when choosing materials. The emphasis here is a compromise between being comparatively light in weight, but having the strength and durability to withstand the wear and tear of more or less constant use throughout the summer. The materials listed next are for building two 3ft × 4ft (91cm × 1.2m) frames. Suitable types of brush material for the filling are discussed at the end of the project.

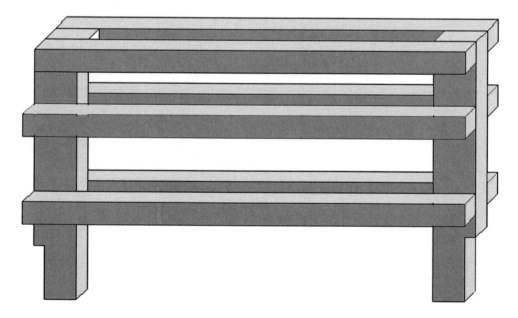

Brush filler.

Material Requirements

- 1 × 12ft (3.6m) × 3in (7.5cm) × 1.75in (4.5cm) treated rail (this will be enough to create 4 × 2.5ft uprights)
- 5 × 12ft (3.6m) × 3in (7.5cm) × 1in (2.5cm) treated rails (four of these are for the horizontal braces that hold the brush in place, with the fifth set aside as a base that stops the material slipping out of the bottom)
- 8 × 4ft (1.2m) × 1in (2.5cm) × 1in (2.5cm) baton (used as flanges to hold the base in position
- A selection of suitably sized wood screws
- Materials for the feet, as described in Chapter 2

Tool Requirements

- Electric drill with suitable bits for the diameter of the bolts and for pilot holes
- Screwdriver
- Wooden mallet
- Suitably sized wrench or socket for the nuts
- Hand saw
- Tri-square
- Pencil
- Tape measure

Method

To create the four uprights, clamp the 12ft × 3in × 1.75in rail to a suitable work area. Using the tape measure, mark four sections of 2.5ft, and scribe four saw guides with the tri-square and pencil. On each of the uprights, cut out halving joints for the feet on the 3in face by following the method described in Chapter 2. Please note: only take out 0.5in–0.75in of depth instead of the full 1in recommended in this chapter, otherwise the frame may snap near the feet. You must leave at least 1in of wood inside the joint channels.

Connecting the horizontal braces is fairly straightforward, but the two bottom rails will require some preparation for batons before you can fix them to the uprights. I suggest you get this job out of the way as quickly as possible. From the 12ft × 3in × 1in rails, saw four 4ft (1.2m) sections. The length of the batons, when in position, will fit between the uprights. The thickness of the uprights, then, must be deducted when measuring the timber. In reality each baton will measure 46.5in (1.18m), so trim them to this size. A quick method of achieving the equation just discussed is to clamp the two batons needed so they run horizontal against both of the uprights. It is then just a simple task of scribing a guideline on the baton using the inside of the uprights as guide.

If any pieces of wood require pilot holes, it will be the 1in × 1in baton, and failing to drill will, without doubt, split the timber beyond any reasonable use. Each baton will need six evenly spaced pilot holes running down their full length to ensure a strong joint. You will also have to determine where on the braces the batons should be fixed. A foolproof method is to align each baton to the bottom edges of their individual braces. Make sure also that you have at least 0.75in (1.9cm) of brace clear at both ends (you will need this much for screwing on to the uprights). Unless you possess the tools to clamp the work properly, I suggest you wait until the bottom braces are connected to the frame before inserting the floor.

The next stage of the project concentrates on joining the braces to the uprights, and you should begin by attaching one complete side first. Lay the uprights on a level work area, then spread them roughly 4ft (1.2m) apart. Take one of the braces, and its attached baton, then place it so that the free 0.75in section of the end rail fits flush with the corresponding 0.75in outer edge of the upright. At this stage the baton should be facing towards the inside of the frame, fitting snugly between the two uprights. Adjust the brace until its bottom edge is resting just above the lip on the foot joint. After drilling a pilot hole, secure it to the frame with a wood screw. Working on the second upright, move it under the brace and secure it in the same fashion. The next brace (one without a baton) is going to be screwed to the very top of the frame. All you have to do here is align the upper

edge of the rail with the top of the two uprights. Again, fix it to the frame with wood screws. Purely for aesthetic reasons, the middle brace will look better if it is secured between the top and bottom ones, leaving an equal space on either side. The measurement to mark is exactly 9in (23cm); measure this from the lower edge of the top timber. Attach the third rail using the guide mark.

You now need to turn the frame upside down to work on the other side. Secure the lower rail and baton as described earlier, but the upper brace should be attached 1in (2.5cm) below the top of the uprights. The reason for the difference is so the horse can see the section behind, helping him to judge the size and width of the obstacle should the brush become dislodged.

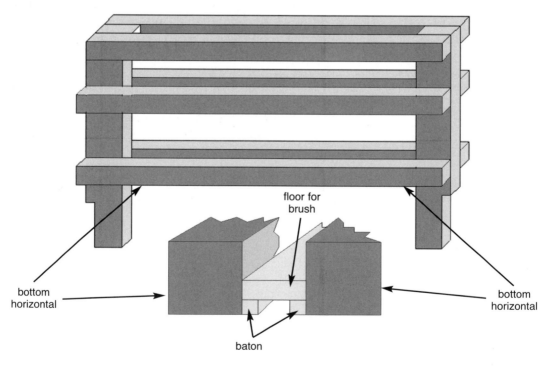

Brush filler.

Before you run out of working space as a result of connecting the centre brace, you should slot in the brush floor between the two timbers at the bottom. Trim this particular timber to at least 1in smaller than the batons at 45.5in (1.15m), otherwise it will jam against the inside of the upright as you lay it down. You may find that you need to gently tap the floor into position with the wooden mallet until it finally comes to rest on the batons. There is no need to screw the floor down, but if you wish to do so, make sure that the pilot holes are drilled in the correct positions. The last thing you want is for the screws to miss the wood completely, which would carry the risk of causing injury.

Attach the middle brace as described for the top and bottom ones, then insert a further screw through each end of every brace. Before connecting the feet, smooth down all sharp corners, and inspect the frame for any protruding hazards. Construct the second brush obstacle using the methods just described.

Choosing Types of Brush

Choosing suitable flora is very important, not least because some foliage is poisonous to equine stock. Avoid using oak, yew, laburnum, privet, laurel and rhododendron if the jump is to be left in a place accessible to horses. The species most commonly used for filling brush jumps is leylandii, but this, too, is not suitable forage, so make sure the horses can't reach it. As a rule, refrain from using ornamental shrubbery. Many trees are unsuitable also, especially the thorny types such as hawthorn and buckthorn. Finding suitable brush shouldn't be that difficult, but try to use foliage from your own property, or seek permission from the landowner first. Deciduous species are ideal for working hunter fences, especially if you want the horse to jump through the branches rather than over them.

Packing the brush jump is straightforward, as it just involves pushing the branches into the frame. Obviously you don't want to leave sharp or jagged branches poking above the top braces. If finding suitable greenstuff proves to be a problem, you can actually purchase plastic foliage – though in my opinion it doesn't seem the right thing to do.

Other Fillers Suitable for a Rustic Jump

Any style filler can be made rustic, it just means that you have to decorate the wood in a natural stain or preservative, rather than colourful paint or bright motifs. A working hunter course is completely made up of rustic wings and fillers, and the good thing is that all of the jumps discussed in this book can easily become part of this group. Common features found in the working hunter arena include the brush jump (just described), gates and a stile. We have already covered the first two in previous chapters, so I am going to end this one by turning the wings into another countryside feature, the wooden stile.

The stile jump, on the working hunter course, is a symbolic example of the real wooden step-over stile found on our public rights-of-way network; all you need is a set of standard wings and 4ft (1.2m) round poles. The narrow access these poles create probably poses one of the most exciting challenges for horse and rider. Chapter 9 contains another idea for designing a stile obstacle.

CHAPTER 6

THE SPREAD JUMP

Whilst a range of spread jumps can be created using two or three sets of wings, it is convenient to have one set that is designed to support a whole spread fence. This minimizes the strain of setting out the course, and makes more effective use of the other wings you own. Out of all the jumps described in this book, I feel this one is most distinctive. The spread jump consists of two wings, each having three sets of uprights: short ones at the front, medium in the centre and tall at the back. Jump cups can be connected to each upright to form a sloping or angled obstacle. The overall height of the jump is relatively small, being only 3ft (91cm) at its highest point, as its challenge is not the height, but the width of the spread. It is relatively simple to construct.

Material Requirements

- 2 × 12ft × 4in × 2in (3.6m × 10cm × 5cm) treated rails (for the uprights)
- 3 × 12ft × 3in × 1in (3.6m × 7.5cm × 2.5cm) treated rails (for the intermediate timbers)
- 8ft of 6in × 2in (15cm × 5cm) board (for the two feet)
- 2 × metal back plates (for securing the feet)
- 4 sets of suitably sized nuts, bolts and washers (for securing the back plates)

- 12 sets of suitably sized nuts, bolts and washers (for connecting the wings together)
- A selection of wood screws

Tool Requirements

- Stable work area (workbench or level area of ground)
- 2 × clamps
- Tape measure
- Tri-square
- Hand saw or electric saw
- Hand drill or electric drill with bits matching the diameter of the bolts and jump-cup pins. Where the jump cups are concerned, it is advisable to use a slightly larger diameter bit than the pin, as it allows the jump cup to be removed and inserted without being forced.
- Wooden mallet
- 1.5in wood chisel
- Screwdriver suitable for the heads of the screws you are using
- Marking pencil

Method of Construction

Before creating the feet as described in Chapter 2, please note that the joint channels should be cut on the wider 4in

Measuring and marking the three uprights needed for one spread jump wing.

Use the tri-square and pencil to mark the saw guidelines.

Sawing through the guidelines to create the uprights.

All six uprights.

face of the uprights. This means that the channels on the feet will have to be made the same width as the uprights' wider 4in faces. Note also that the central uprights do not need to be cut for feet.

Start by securing one of the 12ft × 4in × 2in rails to the work area. With the tape measure and pencil, mark 3.5ft (1.06m) down the length of the timber. Extend the tape measure a further 3ft (0.9m) and mark that point also; then take it another 2.5ft (0.76m), placing a mark again. At each marker, use the tri-square to draw a straight guideline down the timber's 4in face. With your saw, carefully cut through the guides to create the first three uprights. You should now have one

length of timber at 3.5ft, one measuring 3ft in length and an upright of 2.5ft. Saw the second rail using the method just described, and then store all six uprights to one side.

The next phase is to saw the intermediates to their correct sizes. For the time being we will only cut the bottom and middle intermediates: this is because the top rail slopes from back to front and, as suggested in the earlier chapters, it is far easier to trim these sections when aligned with the frame.

Securing a 12ft × 3in × 1in rail to the work area, measure and place a mark at 3ft (91cm), then continue down the timber and scribe another mark, 3.5ft

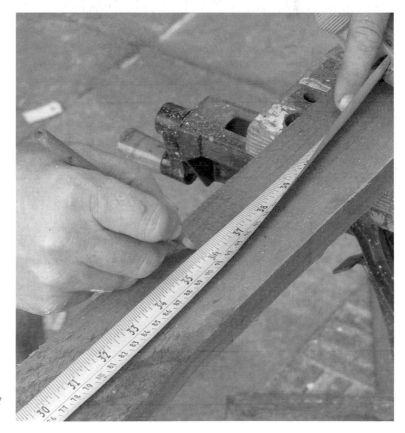

Measuring and marking the intermediates.

Accurately spacing the uprights with the aid of the tape measure.

Checking the length of the wing.

After connecting the bottom horizontal, lay the top intermediate across the frame. Note how the rail overlaps. This overlap can be sawn flush with the outer edges of the uprights.

Attaching the bottom intermediate timber.

Affixing the top diagonal after it has been sawn. Note how the rail end is flush with the outer edge of the upright.

(1.01m) from the first (a total length of 6.5ft (1.98m); the reason for the 0.5in difference will be explained a little later). Draw a guideline, using the tri-square and pencil, through both marks, and then trim carefully with the saw. When you have done this, go back to the uprights and lay them, in height order (tall at the back, medium in the middle and short at the front), on a firm and level surface. Turn each one until they are all resting on their narrow 2in edges, and space them evenly apart. The distance between the tallest and shortest uprights should be no more than 3ft (91cm).

Take a 3ft intermediate and span it across the three uprights. Adjust the rail until one end is flush with the outer edge of either the tallest or shortest uprights, then adjust it until it is resting just above the foot joint. After pre-drilling a pilot hole, connect the intermediate with a wood screw. Moving to the upright at the other end, align and fix the timber in exactly the same way.

To connect the middle portion you first need to work out the halfway point of the entire wing. We already know that the total length of the wing is 3ft, so the centre of the middle upright ought to be

Securing the middle intermediate rail.

secured at 1.5ft. Measure and mark this distance on the intermediate. To help even further, measure 1in either side of this mark and then scribe two lines down the rail's 3in face, with the aid of the tri-square. Next, position the middle upright between these two marks and fine-tune it until it is parallel within the guidelines. Prior to connecting the intermediate, the upright will need to be adjusted so that the bottom is clear of the ground when the wing is erect: you will only have to move it 1in upwards. Rarely will you find a show-jumping arena that is completely level, and if the wing were to rest on three

feet instead of two, the middle one would almost certainly unbalance the whole jump.

The next rail to connect is the top one. This should be laid across the wing so it bridges all three uprights with an overlap either side. Fine-tune the rail so that its top edge bisects the outside top corner of the tall upright, and the inside top corner of the small one. After drilling pilot holes, secure to the frame with wood screws. The angle of the central intermediate is down to personal choice. Some people may prefer to fix it so that it runs parallel with the bottom rail, others may want

The finished wings.

The spread jump painted and ready to go!

to be slightly more creative. As you can see on the project jump, we have subtly blended it with the angle of the top intermediate. If you study the photographs closely you will notice that the middle rail is slightly offset – which is why we measured the timber slightly longer at the beginning of the project. As I said, the choice is up to you. If you have chosen the latter, make sure you leave an overlap for sawing later – the reason why we made this rail slightly longer.

The final major task is drilling and securing the frame with nuts, bolts and washers, and all of the three uprights have to be joined to the intermediate rails in this manner. The last jobs are to attach the feet and to smooth down all the edges.

Construct the second wing in exactly the same manner, remembering that it will be a mirror image of the first.

Fillers

Poles are really all you need for any style of spread. An ascending arrangement of two or three poles is a challenge in its own right.

The spread jump in action.

CHAPTER 7

PILLARS

Perhaps the most appealing set of wings to look at are pillars, their cuboid shape lending itself to any design that takes your fancy; the most obvious variation is a pair of artificial brick pillars, and stretching that concept a little further, you could make a pair of castellated towers to give a hint of the medieval, perhaps with a matching filler. And if the smooth edges of man-made architecture don't appeal, how about a woodland or garden concept? By using trellis in place of one, or two, or maybe three side panels and then adorning the wings with plant forms or natural shapes sawn from plyboard, you will make a jump to be proud of. Indeed, you can make the side panels in whatever shape you please, as long as health and safety parameters are observed.

Of all the wings described in this book, the building of these pillars is the most advanced as far as construction technique is concerned. If you are not sure of your abilities with a mallet and chisel – there are many joints that must be accurately cut – then I suggest you work to the easier method that is discussed later.

Our project jump details the construction of two brick-wall effect pillars, along with a filler of similar pattern. The materials for these pillars reflect the fact that these wings should remain as lightweight as possible, whilst at the same time providing strength and durability – though in the light of this there is no guarantee that they won't be damaged in the unfortunate event of an accident.

Material Requirements

- 4 × 12ft × 3in × 1.75in (3.6m × 7.6cm × 4.5cm) treated rails
- 5 × 12ft × 3in × 1in (3.6m × 7.6cm × 2.5cm) treated rails
- 2 sheets of 8ft × 4ft (2.4m × 1.2m) external plyboard
- PVA wood adhesive
- A selection of suitably sized wood screws

Tool Requirements

- Stable work area (workbench, or level area of ground)
- 2 × clamps
- Tape measure
- Tri-square
- Hand saw or electric saw
- Hand drill or electric drill
- Wooden mallet
- 1.5in wood chisel
- Screwdriver suitable for the heads of the screws you are using
- Marking pencil

Method of Construction

The following pillars are free standing, therefore they do not require feet. To commence, secure one of the 12ft × 3in × 1.75in rails to the work area. Measure and mark a length of 5ft (1.5m) timber, then go on to measure another 5ft section, and finally saw to size. These are the first two uprights for the frames: to simplify matters we will call them 'Timber A' and 'Timber B', and you should mark them as such on one of their faces.

The project relies on eight 5ft uprights, and it may be a good idea to produce these now out of the remaining three rails. There will be some pieces of superfluous timber: keep them safe, as you can use them on the wings to help shore them up later.

Clamp one 5ft upright (A) to the work area, and using the tape measure and pencil, place a mark on the timber at 9in (23cm). Extend the tape a further 3in (7.5cm) (this will be the 1ft mark), and then draw a second mark. Taking the tri-

Joints should be cut on the 3in and 1.75in sides of the uprights.

square, draw one straight line through each mark, across the 3in face of the wood. On both of the rail's 1.75in edges, continue these guidelines a further 0.5in (1.2cm). With a straight edge, join the ends of the guides with a pencil line, to create a depth gauge for sawing. Next, unclamp the work and then turn it so that it rests on the 1.75in edge. With the tri-square aligned to the existing guides, draw another two pencil lines from edge to edge. Concentrating now on the opposite end of the rail, measure and mark 3in (7.5cm), then extend the tape and draw a mark at 6in (15cm). Draw a set of sawing and depth guides exactly as just described.

You now have to cut the joints. Your sawing and chiselling must be extremely accurate if the wings are to stand any chance of appearing true. An ideal scenario will be to use the appropriate machinery, along with its depth gauges, fences and guides, and to have some knowledge of its safe operation. However, some of us will not possess such a tool, and will have to work by hand. Nevertheless, not rushing the job, along with careful use of a hand saw and chisel, will yield perfectly competent results.

Holding the saw steady and horizontal, gently saw down the two guides on the 0.75in edge, to a maximum depth of 0.5in (1.2cm). Do the same for the guides on the opposite end. Next, unclamp the rail and turn it to rest on the 3in face, making sure the guidelines face upwards, and then re-secure to the work area. Working with a steady level saw again, saw down both lines to a maximum depth of 0.5in.

You now need to chisel out channels on the 3in and 0.75in sides of the rail (refer to 'Getting Started', Chapter 1, for advice on using a wooden mallet and chisel). I must stress again that it is always preferable to use the correct cutting machinery, as the depth of all channels must be an exact 0.5in. If you are cutting with a chisel be sure you work in line with the depth gauges, drawn earlier.

The first task with the second upright (Timber B) is to make sure that the joints are cut out on the correct side; to avoid mistakes the simple technique is to lay Timber B alongside Timber A. On Timber A, look for the joints cut into the 1.75in edge, and if they aren't that way already, turn the upright until the joints face towards the outside (this means the 3in face will be facing upwards). Abut Timber B against A, then draw a mark on B's outside edge to highlight the side where you cut the joint. In fact you could do two things at once here: ensure that the ends of both A and B are flush, take the tri-square, align it against the edges of the existing channels, and then, making sure the straight edge crosses on to B, scribe the saw guides on to the new section, across its 3in face. Work to the method described for A when cutting out the joints.

The next upright, Timber C, should be matched with A to enable you to determine the joint areas. Make sure A is resting on its 1.75in edge, with the joint facing up, and then bring C to rest alongside, making sure that the joint on A's 3in side is facing outwards. Line up the timbers until both ends are flush with each other. Take the tri-square and line it with the edges of A's channels (on the 1.75in side), and allow it to cross over on to C, then draw the saw guides. Whilst the two timbers are still in place, highlight C's outward, 3in side to remind you of the fact that this is the face where the next two joints are going to be made.

Again, draw saw guides using the tri-square and pencil.

As this phase of the project is fairly complicated it is wise to recap on the work so far. You should have now created four uprights, A through to D (*see* diagram on page 104); uprights A and B form one pair, uprights C and D also make a pair. It is obvious that all uprights help to form the four corners of the pillar, but it is the orientation of the joints that really matters. With this in mind, be sure that the joint channels of the completed wing always face outwards – the latter is an important fact to remember when affixing the intermediates. To make absolutely certain how these uprights must be positioned in relation to the intermediates, stand A edge to edge with B (0.75in) so that the joints match. Looking down the narrow side of the timber, turn one upright until both timbers are back to back. You will now notice that all the channels face outwards. Depending on which perspective you perceive, A now becomes the front right upright, B is now the back right one. With the pencil, mark a reminder on both timbers. Now do the

Sawing through the intermediate's 3in guideline.

same with uprights D and C, remembering the joints go on the outside.

Now move on to the 12ft × 3in × 1in rails. For one pillar you will require a total of eight 2ft-long (60cm) timbers. One 12ft rail is only enough for six intermediates, so two more must be sawn off another rail. Securing the work firmly, measure and mark 2ft intervals down the first rail. With the help of the tri-square, draw the usual saw guides in pencil, and then saw to size. Secure the second rail, cutting the last two intermediates in the same fashion. We now have the eight timbers for the first pillar. Although their lengths are equal, half of them will have a different-sized 'cut-out' for the halving joint.

We will first concentrate on the sections that join Timber A to Timber B. Notice that the intermediates have to cross the 3in sides of both uprights; the joint must be made to suit. When the intermediate has been clamped to the work area, take the tape measure and measure 3in (7.6cm) from one end, draw a mark, and scribe a guideline using the tri-square and pencil. Repeat the same at the opposite end. Working at both ends in turn, create a depth line on the 1in edge of no more than 0.5in. Holding the saw

Applying a layer of PVA adhesive to Timber A's joint.

Slotting the intermediate into the upright's joint.

Screwing the intermediate to the upright.

Accurate, flush joints.

horizontal, slowly cut through the 3in guide until the teeth just touch the depth guide. Again, repeat this at the other end. The next job is best carried out with the timber held vertically in a vice, as you need to very carefully saw down the depth guide until you reach the first cut. By then the waste wood should come away easily. Repeat for the opposite end. Follow exactly the same method for the second intermediate rail.

It is now time to join Timbers A and B. Lay both uprights on a level work area, and space them roughly 2ft (60cm) apart. Ensure that the joints on both uprights correspond, and that they face outwards, then spread a layer of PVA adhesive into each channel. Slot the end of one intermediate into one of A's channels, gently tapping home with the wooden mallet. Drill two pilot holes and drive in two woodscrews. Affix the second intermediate into A's second channel. To avoid disturbing the rails, align Timber B and attach the intermediates in the same fashion. Join Timbers C and D following the method just described; then leave to dry.

This next stage deals with joining Timbers A to C and B to D. The cut-outs on the remaining four rails are now measured at 0.75 as opposed to 3in, to allow them to cross the narrow sides of the uprights; that difference apart, measuring, marking and sawing are the same. To actually join the frames it is advisable to enlist a friend to help hold the work whilst you push the intermediates into the joint channels. After connecting the first side, the frame must be turned upside down to affix the last rails. Please be careful when performing this, because the pillar is still fragile at this stage. Apart from the latter, building the second pillar is an exact replication of the process just described.

As an added feature of strength you can enhance the pillars by inserting diagonal braces inside the frames. These are short sections of rail that bridge the intermediates on each corner. There should be ample waste left over from the rails used to make the intermediates; they are ideal for this next job. To start, take one length and bridge the intermediates on the inside of one corner, pushing the rail against the upright. Working from underneath and on the outside of the frame, draw a straight pencil line, using the intermediate as a straight edge. Repeat this on the opposite side of the offcut. You should now see two diagonal saw guides.

Attaching the braces to help strengthen the pillar.

Once the brace has been clamped and sawn to size, place it back on the frame, adjusting if necessary to ensure a flush fit on the outside. Drill pilot holes, and connect with wood screws. Repeat the procedure for the remaining corners, top and bottom.

Before we proceed I would just like to explain that the only viable method of using jump cups is to attach factory-made strips that run vertically down the centre of one side — more on this later. Since we are trying to keep this project lightweight and portable, the strips depicted on the jump here are just screwed to the panel and intermediates. If, however, your pillars are going to sustain heavy usage, such as at shows throughout the season, where many riders use the wings, additional vertical struts must be added to the inside of each wing to anchor the jump-cup strips. For personal light use the strips can be screwed direct to the panel, but to be on the safe side you may want to add one anyway.

Attaching the Side Panels

Each pillar will require four side panels of 2ft (0.6m) × 4ft (1.2m), which can be

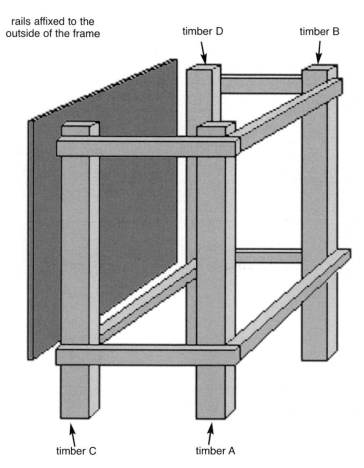

rails affixed to the outside of the frame

timber D

timber B

timber C

timber A

Alternative method of construction for a pillar wing.

sawn from one 8ft (2.4m) × 4ft (1.2m) plyboard. To work comfortably, the plyboard is best laid on a raised workspace offering a large enough surface area. Failing this, most DIY retailers will cut the sizes you require. Please also refer to Chapter 4 for instructions on how to accurately saw the board into 2ft × 4ft panels, and the technique for screwing them on to the frames.

Let us assume your pillars will have to tolerate heavy use, in which case you may need to add an extra timber to help affix the jump strip. Find the centre of the pillar by working out the measurement between uprights A and C; place a mark on the top and bottom horizontals. Next, measure the distance between the top and bottom horizontals, and then highlight it on a length of rail before sawing to size. Lining the centre of the rail with marks on the horizontals, gently push the rail between the two. In addition to the usual fixing screws (*see* Chapter 4), a third vertical row is driven in to secure the strut; it must be attached to the horizontals with either brackets or angled nails.

Fixing on a plyboard panel.

One completed pillar frame.

The finished pillar. All it needs is some décor.

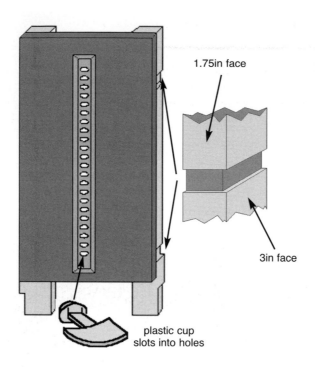

1.75in face

3in face

Rectangle wing showing jump-cup strip, cup and joints.

plastic cup slots into holes

rail for affixing jump-cup strip

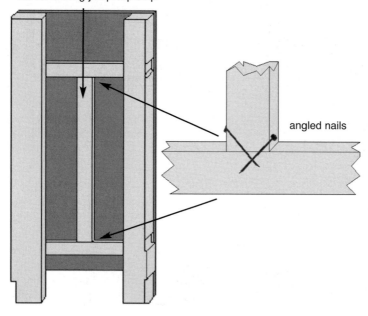

angled nails

Pillar wing from behind showing rail for affixing the jump-cup strip.

Alternative Method of Pillar Construction

This method is an alternative to using halving joints, although the following design, albeit adequate, will not produce a frame of the same quality as our main project wings. For the most part, all timbers are sized as explained before; the only change of technique is that the rails are just fixed to the outside of the frame. As easy as it sounds, it may not be straightforward if you happen to be working without assistance. Without halving joints holding timbers in place, you will be dogged by the constant movement of the pillar until such time as you can affix corner braces and side panels. Another drawback is the chance that the plyboard will fail to cover the whole frame unless you are prepared to purchase a little extra (although the shortfall will amount to inches rather than feet, affecting appearance rather than strength).

The alternative method of constructing the pillar. Note that the intermediates are attached to the outside of the frame. Whilst this design is easier to build, its disadvantages are numerous: you will have to continually align the frame, it is somewhat cumbersome to manoeuvre until braced, and the aesthetic finish is not as elegant as one constructed with joints.

Alternative Pillar Styles

The principal benefit of building pillars is that a much greater choice of design is available. A cuboid shape may seem dull and boring, but the ethos behind any design is to transform the bland into the interesting. Although the important factors here are safety and functionality, I hope I can suggest one or two ideas that may inspire you to more wondrous arrangements.

Trellis Pillars (rustic)

These pillars have the potential to brighten up any show-jumping arena. Built around the frame described for this chapter's main project jump, trellis sections can be attached instead of plyboard panels. By adding a floor and top section you can adorn the pillars with plants to add colour and vibrancy. To minimize the risk of a hoof getting trapped or a leg injured, at least one ply panel will need to be affixed to the region where the jump-cup strip is fastened.

Material Requirements
The majority of materials are as listed for the project jump, but with the following changes:

- 3 × 2ft (0.6m) × 4ft (1.2m) exterior plyboard panels (two boards are used in conjunction with jump-cup strips, the last one sawn into four 2ft × 2ft shelves)
- 6 × 2ft (0.6m) × 4ft (1.2m) trellis panels (these can be purchased from garden suppliers in the sizes mentioned)
- Wood preservative of relevant colour

Tool Requirements
As listed for the project jump.

Method of Construction
Follow the procedures described for the project jump. Once you have built the frames, join the plyboard and two trellis panels in the same fashion. Before joining the third trellis, measure the frame for its floor and top shelf. The framework, as you already know, is 2ft × 2ft. To work out the size of shelving required, multiply the length by the width; in this case the equation comes to 4ft squared. You will also have to make allowances for the uprights, and cut the plyboard to fit accordingly. I suggest that the shelves should be screwed into position, especially the top one. Once in place, the last trellis can be connected.

A variety of artificial plants can be purchased to fill the pillars: these have the advantage of being able to withstand constant use – and they don't rot. During the summer months a wide choice of natural species will become available. However, be careful not to choose poisonous items just in case the horse pulls up and takes a bite. Research the plants you can and cannot use.

Fillers and Rails

One's own imagination is far superior to another's ideas, particularly as there is no accounting for personal taste. I can specify some basic designs, which you could enhance with an individual statement.

Free-Standing Wall Filler

This type of filler is used in conjunction with a pole or poles that is/are hung from jump cups above the filler. In this design the wall obstacle complements the brick-style pillars built as the project jump. Like the brush filler described in Chapter 5, it consists of two sections of 2ft (0.6m) × 4ft (1.2m). The height, of course, can be changed at the constructional stage to suit riders of differing abilities; the height of the jump can also be raised by adding poles above the filler.

Material Requirements

The materials used reflect the need to keep the feature as lightweight as possible: it is therefore only 3in thick.

- 3 × 12ft (3.6m) × 3in (7.5cm) × 1.75in (4.5cm) treated rails
- 1 × 8ft (2.4m) × 4ft (1.2m) plyboard panel (you will need to saw this into four panels of 2ft (0.6m) × 4ft (1.2m))
- 8ft (2.4m) of 6in (15cm) × 2in (5cm) board (for the feet)
- 2 × metal back plates
- 4 × suitably sized nuts, bolts and washers (to secure the back plates to the feet)
- A selection of wood screws
- PVA adhesive

Tool Requirements

As listed for the project jump.

Method of Construction

Construct the feet as described in Chapter 2, ensuring the joint channels are cut to 3in in width. Next, you will need to saw all the rails to the sizes and quantities required. These are as follows (the size of the ply panels has already been stated): four of 2.5ft (0.76m), and four of 4ft (1.2m).

Unlike the wing uprights, the feet sections on the wall do not require chiselled joint areas, as this may weaken the structure. Instead, the 3in faces of the rails

slot directly into the channels on the feet. However, the vertical end rails do depend on joints to hold the lower horizontal timbers.

Assuming that the rails are now sawn to specification, begin by clamping one 2.5ft timber on to the work area. Working with the 3in face, measure 6in from one end, and mark with a pencil. Extend this measurement a further 0.75in and draw a second mark. With the aid of the tri-square, draw a straight guideline, bisecting each marker, across the 3in face of the workpiece. On both sides of the rail create a depth line of about 1in deep. Working carefully, saw through the guides on the 3in face, stopping when the teeth are just touching the depth gauge. Taking the mallet and chisel, cut away the waste section between the saw guides (*refer* to Chapter 1, 'Getting Started', for advice on using a chisel). Repeat this method on the remaining three end rails, and apply a layer of PVA adhesive inside the joints.

The next job is to slot a lower horizontal into the joints. It may require a little persuasion with the wooden mallet, in which case you may need some assistance in holding the work. Now you have the horizontal in the joint, drive in four wood-screws, two through each end of the frame; these will help to strengthen the joints. At present the frame is very flimsy, and connecting a top rail may disturb the joints. As a temporary holding action, span the two uprights by screwing on an extra length of wood, ensuring that the uprights remain 4ft apart. To be on the safe side, leave the frame to dry according to the PVA adhesive manufacturer's instructions.

Connecting the top rail will be easier if you slot on the feet and secure them to the frame; you can then use the ground as

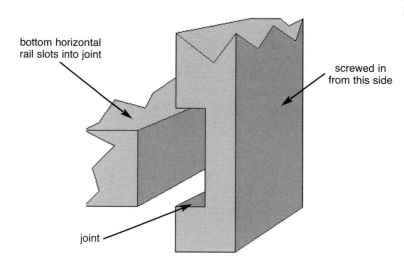

bottom horizontal
rail slots into joint

*Showing the joint for the
lower horizontal rail on
the wall filler frame.*

screwed in
from this side

joint

a buttress to help with the next job. Taking one 4ft section of rail, place it on top of both vertical sections. With the drill, bore out four pilot holes (two at each end) and secure it with screws, making sure the work is flush on the external sides. Now remove the holding brace.

You will have to remove the feet when connecting the two side panels. Basically this next phase is a repeat of the method described in Chapter 4 for attaching the plyboards, but you will find that the panels do not fully cover the edge of the top rail – this is by design, and is not an error. Most real walls are built with two skins, and top stones or coping are then laid to bridge these faces, tying the structure together. By leaving the majority of top rail exposed, you create a contrast with the frame's smooth sides; this contrast can be maximized by painting on coping. To conclude, build the second wall using the technique just described.

Palisade

The palisade is a very popular obstacle, found on most show-jumping and working hunter courses. What is more, it suits both rustic and decorated wings.

Material Requirements
- 3 × 12ft (3.6m) × 3in (7.5cm) × 1in (2.5cm) treated rails
- 4 sets of suitably sized nuts, bolts and washers
- A selection of wood screws

Tool Requirements
- Hammer
- Screwdriver
- Drill complete with suitable bits for the diameter of bolts and for drilling pilot holes for screws
- Hacksaw
- Sanding block or electric sander

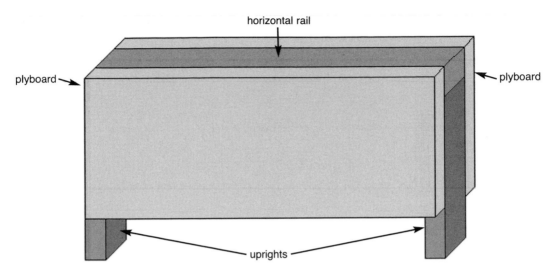

A wall filler.

Method of Construction

Take one 12ft (3.6m) × 3in (7.5cm) × 1in (2.5cm) rail and secure it to the workbench. Measuring from one end, place a mark at 8ft (2.4m), and saw to size. Whilst you are working on this rail, saw off a length of 3ft (0.9m), and put it aside for later use. Working with the second 12ft rail, measure and mark 7.5ft (2.3m) and another 3ft, then saw to size also. Put aside the new 3ft section with the first. Turning your attention again to the 8ft rail, measure 3in (7.5cm) from one end, and then draw a straight line down the 3in face, using the tri-square as an aid. Now do exactly the same at the opposite end of the rail. The two guidelines represent the outside edge of the palisade frame, whereas the two 3in overlaps are the hangers for resting on jump cups. To continue, take the third rail and mark four measurements of 3ft. After drawing the respective sawing guides, cut them down to size. You have now made the 8ft top rail, the 7.5ft bottom rail, and the six 3ft, vertical intermediate timbers.

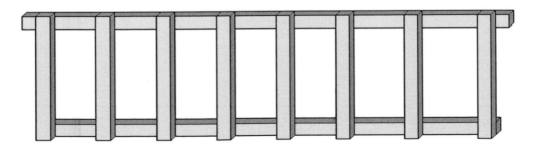

A palisade filler.

Now we can put the whole thing together. Lay the 8ft horizontal rail on level ground, then take one 3ft vertical intermediate and align it with the inside of a guideline (drawn earlier for the hanger). Making sure the edge of the intermediate is parallel with this line, affix it to the 8ft, using wood screws driven through pilot holes. Take a second 3ft timber and do the same at the opposite end of the horizontal. Now working with the 7.5ft rail, push it underneath the ends of the connected intermediates (not the end with the 8ft rail). Adjust the horizontal until both ends are flush with the vertical timbers. You may find you'll have to tweak the verticals as well. Next, screw the intermediates in place.

It is important that the frame isn't lop-sided and remains true throughout the building phase. You can check this by measuring the diagonals, from the top right corner to the bottom left-hand corner, and then do the same from the top left to the bottom right. If both measurements are the same, the frame is true. When you are satisfied, the remaining intermediates can be connected. Aesthetically speaking, the palisade will look more appealing if the gaps between the verticals are equal. The final job, apart from smoothing down all the rough edges, is to drill the four corners, then firm up with nuts, bolts and washers.

The finished pillar jump in action.

CHAPTER 8

RECTANGLE TRELLIS WINGS

They say that variety is the spice of life, and certainly there is no better place to incorporate it but in a set of show jumps. The rectangle trellis is an attractive yet easy feature to build, and one that is equally at home on working hunter and show-jumping arenas. Small, sturdy, and designed to stand the test of time, this one will give you immense pleasure. The project specified here has a maximum height of 4ft (1.2m) and a width of 3ft (0.9m). The trellis structures, unlike the pillars described in Chapter 7, are assembled by joining individual lengths of 2in (5cm) × 2in rail (or lats), and as you can see, are a statement of durability. They should be used in conjunction with jump-cup strips.

Material Requirements

- 4 × 4ft (1.2m) × 4in (10cm) × 2in (5cm) treated uprights
- 1 × 12ft (3.6m) × 3in (7.5cm) × 1.75in (4.5cm) treated rail for the intermediates
- 6 × 12ft (3.6m) × 2in (5cm) × 2in treated rails
- 4 × 2ft (0.6m) × 6in (15cm) × 2in (5cm) boards for the feet
- 2 back plates

- 4 sets of suitable size nuts, bolts and washers for securing the feet
- 8 sets of suitable size nuts, bolts and washers for connecting the wings
- A selection of screws
- 2 jump-cup strips

Tool Requirements

- Stable work area (workbench or level area of ground)
- 2 clamps
- Tape measure
- Tri-square
- Hand saw or electric saw
- Hand drill or electric drill
- Wooden mallet
- 1.5in wood chisel
- Screwdriver suitable for the heads of the screws you are using
- Marking pencil

Method of Construction

First make the feet as described in Chapter 2, and cut the second parts of the halving joints on all four uprights. Next, lay two uprights on a level work area, roughly 3ft (0.9m) apart. Making sure that the joints face towards the outside, place one 3ft intermediate to span the two timbers, and bring its bottom edge in line with the halving joint's lip on both uprights. Before fixing with screws, check that the ends of the rail are flush with the outer edges of the wing. Working from the opposite end of the uprights, measure 1in down the 4in face of both sections, and then place a mark on each. With the tri-square and pencil, bisect these marks with two guidelines across the 4in faces. Span the uprights using a second inter-mediate, ensuring its top edge is just touching the guidelines. Again, check to see if the outside of the wing is flush, and move the uprights to line up with the end of the rails if necessary. Drill pilot holes and affix the rail to the frame using wood screws.

The next stage is to make the trellis section's lats. Due to the quantity of rail, be prepared for intensive pilot hole drilling. First, you will need to saw the 12ft × 2in × 2in rails to make the individual trellis sections: seven of 3ft (0.9m) for the horizontals, and five of 3ft for the ver-

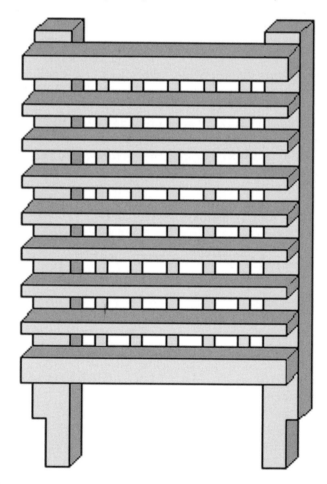

A rectangle trellis wing.

tical intermediates. You should also make two spacers, one 2in (5cm) long and the other 3in (7.5cm) long.

Always, and throughout the project, ensure that the lats are flush with the outside faces of the wing. To begin, take the 3in spacer and lay it on an upright, then abut one end against the top edge of the lower horizontal. Taking one 3ft lat, place its bottom edge against the spacer's top, and fix it to the frame using wood screws. Move the spacer across to the next upright, and repeat. You should now have a 3in gap between the bottom rail and the first lat. Continue in this fashion until you have connected eight horizontal lats.

The next stage is to join the vertical lats. First, turn the wing upside down, preferably on something soft like an old blanket to protect the timber. Still using the 3in spacer, position it on the top horizontal rail and abut to the upright's edge. Take the first vertical lat, and attach it as previously described. Move the spacer to the bottom of the frame and secure the vertical there. Now connect the remaining lats with the aid of the 2in spacer. Note that the space between the last lat and upright will be roughly 3in.

Now connect all the lats to each other. Using the drill, bore pilot holes where each timber crosses another: you will need about seventy-two in total. The size of screw is also important: use a shank of no more than 2.5in long. The construction of the second wing follows exactly the same method.

Perhaps you can't be bothered with measuring and sawing seemingly endless lengths of rail, or you just want to minimize the overall weight of the finished product. However, although purchasing ready-made trellis may seem a viable option, be aware that shop-bought trellis may not be heavy duty, and would be quite likely to splinter in the event of an accident; it is therefore much safer to make up the trellis yourself.

Fillers and Rails

The trellis filler is based around the same frame as described in Chapter 7 for the wall, the obvious difference being that lats are used instead of plyboard. The overall weight is an important consideration, given that the structure mustn't be too heavy to carry about. Use the palisade filler instructions, described in Chapter 7, adding a few extra horizontal 2in × 2in timbers so that the design complements the wings. This will ensure a lighter filler. You may be tempted to use shop-bought trellis for making a quick, lightweight filler, but don't: if a horse put a foot through this sort of trellis, it might cause lacerations to its lower leg and put a stop to your training schedule for weeks.

Material Requirements

As listed for the palisade filler described earlier, plus two 7.5ft × 2in × 2in timbers.

Tool Requirements

As described in Chapter 7.

Method of Construction

The main frame is constructed in the same way as the one for the palisade filler. Fixing on the extra horizontal rails is a simple task of drilling pilot holes and screwing in screws.

CHAPTER 9

STILE JUMP

Rustic stile wings definitely look the part on a working hunter course, and are just as neat in the show-jumping arena, painted in any colour you like. The jump resembles a field boundary, with each wing representing a post and rail fence. The filler, which is merely there for effect and to act as some form of groundline, is the stile tread. The equestrian connection is the pole that hangs between the wings.

Material Requirements

- 2 × 5ft (1.5m) × 4in (10cm) × 2in (5cm) uprights
- 2 × 3ft (0.9m) × 4in (10cm) × 2in (5cm) uprights
- 2 × 12ft (3.6m) × 3in (7.6cm) × 1in (2.5cm) treated rails (you actually only require one-and-a-half lengths of rail, but you will probably have to buy them in two full sections, depending on the goodwill of your supplier)
- 4 × 2ft (0.6m) × 6in (15cm) × 2in (5cm) boards for the feet
- 8 nuts, bolts and washers of suitable size
- A selection of wood screws of suitable size

Tool Requirements

- Stable work area (workbench or level area of ground)
- Two clamps
- Tape measure
- Tri-square
- Hand saw or electric saw
- Hand drill or electric drill
- Wooden mallet
- 1.5in wood chisel
- Screwdriver suitable for the heads of the screws you are using
- Marking pencil

Method of Construction

Create the feet as described in Chapter 2; cut the second parts of the foot joints on all four uprights, then drill the jump-cup pin holes, using the template as described in the chapter 'Getting Started'.

To begin, measure and saw the 12ft × 3in × 1in rail into six 3ft (0.9m) lengths; then place them to one side. Next, take one of the 5ft (1.5m) uprights and lay it down on a level surface. Working from the top, mark a measurement of 2ft (0.6m), then create a straight guideline

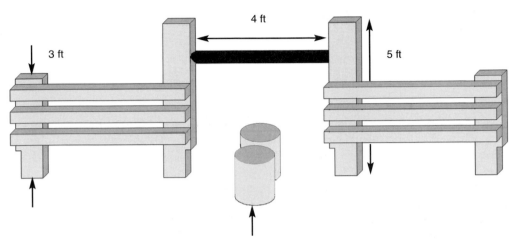

3 ft

4 ft

5 ft

tread uprights waiting for half-round rails

Stile jump and fillers.

across the upright's 4in face with the aid of the tri-square and pencil. Next, bring one of the 3ft uprights into play, and lay it side by side against the 5ft one; ensuring that the foot joints face outwards, move them roughly 3ft apart. Working with one 3ft rail, position it across the uprights, moving it into line with the lip of the foot joints. Ensuring that both ends are even with the outside of the wings, drill pilot holes for the screws and affix to the frame. Take a second 3ft rail and align its top edge with the 2ft guideline on the tall timber (marked earlier) and the very top of the smaller 3ft upright. Screw the rail down, and check that the maximum distance between each upright

remains at 3ft.

The third rail is affixed between the top and bottom horizontals, and for the wing to look right, you should attach it right in the centre. The actual centre point is 15in (30cm), after measuring vertically between the inside of both rails. Once you have done that, screw the rail on as normal. The wing is now rigid, but to further secure the frame, add another screw to each fixing point. When you have attached the feet, check the frame for sharp protrusions and smooth down all acute edges. Build the second wing following the instructions just described, remembering that it is a mirror image of the first.

Stile Tread Filler

A stile wouldn't be a stile without a tread, though in our case it only acts as a symbolic representation. You cannot, of course, add proper stile steps, firstly because they are too big, and secondly they pose a risk to horse and rider.

Material Requirements

- 2 × 2ft × 6in (60cm × 15cm) treated round posts
- 2 × 2ft × 3in (60cm × 7.5cm) treated half-round rails
- 8 × 5in (127mm) nails
- 2 metal angle brackets (optional)

Tool Requirements

- Hammer
- Saw
- Sanding block, electrical sander or surform rasp

Method of Construction

This construction won't take up much of your time at all. Start by standing up the 2ft round posts, and place them roughly 2ft apart. Take the two lengths of half-round rail and lay them side by side across both uprights, ensuring a flush fit at both ends. Drill eight pilot holes, two for each rail-end, then hammer in the eight 5in nails. In additional you can make the step more rigid by attaching two large angle brackets underneath the rails.

The stile must be used with a jump pole or board, with the tread standing diagonally below. The step is purely ornamental and should not impede the safe use of the jump.

CHAPTER 10

BUILDING YOUR JUMPING COURSE

Now you have made a set of show jumps you will undoubtedly be eager to try them out. However, I will only cover basic safety information here, as the remit of this book was to cover construction. When you build your jumping course, the prime consideration is the safety of horse, rider and any spectator who may be watching from the sidelines. Apart from having a great deal of fun, the fundamental basics of a jumping course is to test the level of ability of both animal and rider, and how the rider communicates with his or her mount. Human and horse form a partnership, but the jumps are there to test the horse's ability, balance and courage, and this can only be safely accomplished on a course that suits the proficiency of both parties.

Your show jumps should be set out with regard to many factors, such as the ground conditions, the weather, the size of the arena (or grass enclosure) and the level of the riders' skill and the horses' ability. Check for hidden dangers on the ground: look for items such as rocks and sharp stones within the landing areas,

and avoid standing the jumps on hummocks, dips and steep slopes. Also look out for external factors that may cast shadows or cause distractions.

You should ensure that you are experienced and competent before attempting to build or tackle a course of show jumps. Setting up jumps at inappropriate distances or at peculiar angles can actually be dangerous and detrimental to a horse and rider's progress. I cannot emphasize more strongly the importance of proper instruction from a qualified trainer at all levels.

The remit of this book is not to teach you how to set up a show-jumping arena, but to explain to you the principles behind constructing the actual jumps themselves. If you wish to learn the skills of course building and all that it entails, many riding centres and further education establishments run certificated courses, and it may be worth contacting them. On the other hand, the book market is filled with some excellent guides for this specific purpose.

CHAPTER 11

SERVICING OLD SHOW JUMPS

You may already own a set of show jumps, and all you want to do is build an extra one or two, using the ideas this book has to offer. Before embarking on these projects it is advisable to inspect your old jumps, checking them for wear and tear. This is vitally important where old constructions are concerned, as the quality of wood treatments when these were probably built may not have been of the high standards demanded today.

The obvious areas to inspect are the places where no air can circulate, such as the joints between two sections of timber. This is where pockets of moisture will have collected, beginning the decaying process. A very common site of deterioration is where the jump touches the ground, and specifically, the joints between the jump's uprights and feet: this can seriously undermine the obstacle's ability to keep upright, and a collapse here could expose all manner of sharp, rusty fixings at the same level as the horse's fetlocks.

Other points to inspect are the existing screws and bolts, along with their pilot holes; these will inevitably be rusty, and the wood surrounding them either rotten or expanded away from the fixing's threads – the slightest knock could bring the show jump crashing down on horse and rider. Where pilot holes have become worn, try drilling new ones, then reconnect the structure with new, rust-resistant fittings.

Sometimes rot will be hidden under layers of old paint, and the only way to check it is by pushing a screwdriver, or similar, into the timber. In severe cases you will be able to push the screwdriver a long way, like forcing a stick into soft sand. My advice here is to discard the jump and build a new one. This type of damage is not just limited to show-jump wings, because fillers like gates and the frames for brushes can all suffer the same fate. Safety, as mentioned earlier, is very important, and to continually patch up worn material in an attempt to save money could ultimately lead to an expensive vet's bill. The best way to avoid or minimize this type of degeneration is to store the jumps under cover with the feet taken off, thus ensuring there is an adequate air supply around the timber at all times. If storing under cover isn't an option, then building jumps using the timber described for this book's projects (wood treated for outdoor use) will help to reduce all the complications associated with mildew, fungus and other forms of decomposition.

To preserve your constructions even further, a regime of general maintenance and inspection should be instigated regularly. Jobs to carry out are:

- Inspect pilot holes for wear. Applying light, clean oil will help to lubricate screws and bolts, and will protect the wood surrounding them.
- After each use, check the security of screws, nuts and bolts. Tighten if loose. This procedure is essential if a wing or filler has been stamped on, or has collided with a horse or pony.
- Use a non-toxic wood preservative on joints, and paint it on at least twice a year (depending on use and where they are stored).
- When re-painting wings, try to remove as much of the old covering as possible. Too many layers may hide future decay problems.
- Apply non-toxic wood preservative on rustic wings and fillers at least twice a year (depending on use and where they are stored).

- After each use, clean mud and dust off wings and feet.
- If jumps have to be left outside, ensure they are stored in the corner of a manège or in a fenced-off section of field separate from grazing areas where equines could possibly injure themselves or damage the jumps.

Recycling Old Fixings

In the case of a worn-out show jump, all is not totally lost, since nuts and bolts can be re-used as long as the threads aren't bare and the shanks are straight. The back plates and fixings for the feet as discussed in this book are very common, and many jumps, old and new, will be using them. It is advisable to save these for your new wings. Screws, though, are a different matter and in my experience I have found it is always better to purchase new. Rusty bolts can be made serviceable by soaking them in clean oil, and perhaps a clean with a wire brush. Corroded screws will almost certainly be useless. The wing's main upright, although rotten, can serve as an ideal template for the new jump-cup pin holes.

USEFUL ADDRESSES

Related Statutory Organizations

Central Council of Physical Recreation
Francis House
Francis Street
London SW1P 1DE
Tel: 0207 828 3163/4
Fax: 0207 630 8820

Countryside Agency
John Dower House
Crescent Place
Cheltenham
Gloucestershire GL50 3RA
Tel: 01242 521381
Fax: 01242 584270

Countryside Council for Wales
Plas Penrhos
Fford Penrhos
Bangor
Gwynedd LL57 2LQ
Tel: 01248 370444

Environment Agency
Rio House
Waterside Drive
Aztec West
Almondsbury
Bristol BS12 4UD
Tel: 01454 624400
Fax: 01454 624409

Forestry Commission
231 Corstorphine Road
Edinburgh EH12 7AT
Tel: 0131 334 0303
Fax: 0131 334 3047

Irish Sports Council
21 Fitzwilliam Square
Dublin 2

Sports Council for Northern Ireland
Tel: 028 90381222

Sports Council for Wales
Tel: 029 20300500

Sport Scotland
Tel: 0131 317 7200

UK Sport
Tel: 0207 841 9500
email: info@uksport.gov.uk

Related Equine Organizations

British Equestrian Federation
National Agricultural Centre
Stoneleigh Park
Kenilworth
Warks CV8 2RH
Tel: 024 7669 8871
Fax: 024 7669 6484

British Equestrian Vaulting
47 Manderley Close
Eastern Green
Coventry CV5 7NR
Tel: 024 7646 3027

British Eventing
National Agricultural Centre
Stoneleigh Park
Kenilworth
Warks CV8 2RN
Tel: 024 7669 8856
Fax: 024 7669 7235
email: info@britisheventing.com

British Show Jumping Association
National Agricultural Centre
Stoneleigh Park
Kenilworth
Warks CV8 2LR
Tel: 024 7669 8800
Fax: 024 7669 6685
email: bsja@bsja.co.uk

Country Landowners Association
16 Belgrave Square
London SW1X 8PQ
Tel: 0207 235 0511
Fax: 0207 235 4696
email: mail@cla.org.uk

Countryside Alliance
The Old Town Hall
367 Kennington Road
London SE11 4PT
Tel: 0207 840 9200
Fax: 0207 793 8899
email: info@countryside-alliance.org

Equestrian Security Services (Freeze Marking)
17 St Johns Road
Farnham
Surrey GU9 8NU
Tel: 01252 727053
Fax: 01252 737738

Equine Behaviour Forum
Grove Cottage
Brinkley
Newmarket
Suffolk CB8 0SF
Tel: 01638 507502
Fax: 01772 786037
email: f.l.burton@udcf.glasgow.ac.uk

Equine Grass Sickness Fund
The Moredun Foundation
Pentlands Science Park
Bush Loan
Penicuik
Midlothian EH26 0PZ
Tel: 0131 445 6257/5111
Fax: 0131 445 6235
email: equine@mf.mri.sari.ac.uk

Farriers Registration Council
Sefton House
Adams Court
Newark Road
Peterborough
Cambs PE1 5PP
Tel: 01733 319911
Fax: 01733 319910
email: frc@farrier-reg.gov.uk

Guild of Master Craftsman
166 High Street
Lewes
East Sussex BN7 1XU
Tel: 01273 477374
Fax: 01273 478606
Contact: Information Officer

International League for the Protection of Horses
Anne Colvin House
Hall Farm
Snetterton
Norwich
Norfolk NR16 2LR
Tel: 01953 498682
Fax: 01953 498373

National Association of Farriers, Blacksmiths & Agricultural Engineers
Avenue B, 10th Street
National Agricultural Centre
Stoneleigh Park
Kenilworth
Warks CV8 2LG
Tel: 024 7669 6595
Fax: 024 7669 6708
email: nafbaehq@nafbae.co.uk

National Equine Welfare Council
Stanton
10 Wales Street
Kings Sutton, Nr Banbury
Oxon OX17 3RR
Tel/Fax: 01295 810 060
email: newc@kingssutton.freeserve.co.uk

North Shropshire and Walford College
Baschurch
Shrewsbury
Shropshire SY4 2HL
Tel: 01939 262100

The Open College of Equine Science
Tel: 01284 700703
email: enquiries@equinestudies.co.uk

Open Spaces Society
25a Bell Street
Henley-on-Thames
Oxon RG9 2BA
Tel: 01491 573535

ThePony Club
National Agricultural Centre
Stoneleigh Park
Kenilworth
Warks CV8 2RW
email: enquiries@pcuk.org
Tel: 024 7669 8300
Fax: 024 7669 6836
Berwyn and Dee Branch
http://www.berwynanddee.co.uk

Pony Riders Association
22 Berry's Road
Upper Bucklebury
Reading
Berks RG7 6QN
Tel: 01635 867891

RSPCA
The Causeway
Horsham
West Sussex RH12 1HG
Tel: 01403 264181
Fax: 01403 241048
email: veterinary@rspca.org.uk

Society for the Welfare of Horses and Ponies
Coxstone
St Maughans
Monmouth NP5 3QF
Tel: 01600 750233
Fax: 01600 750468
email: swhp@swhp.co.uk

Welsh Trekking & Riding Association
118 Beacons Park
Brecon
Powys CF14 5GG
Tel: 01874 622521

GLOSSARY

Brush jump: Obstacle designed to imitate a natural hedgerow.

Filler: Free-standing obstacle normally used in conjunction with rails and jump poles. Fillers can be constructed to hold foliage for brush jumps or to resemble a wall, to give but two examples.

Gate: Obstacle based on the agricultural field gate, designed to sit between a set of wings.

Intermediate: Used in this book to describe all timber sections excluding feet and uprights, but including vertical, horizontal and diagonal rails.

Jump cup: Metal or plastic fitting designed to hold rails and poles.

Jump-cup pin: Fitting that holds a jump cup to a wing, usually pushed through a hole on an upright.

Jump-cup strip: Long section of metal or plastic for holding safe jump cups.

Jump pole: Cylindrical piece of wood that horse and rider jump.

Palisade: Obstacle resembling a palisade fence. Usually hangs between a set of wings, but can also be free standing.

Pillar: Box-effect wing with four decorated side panels.

Rail: Obstacle hung between wings, usually a board.

Rectangle wing: Unlike the standard wing, which contains one tall upright and one short upright, the rectangle has two of the same size. Normally comes panelled, but many different designs have been used.

Standard wing. The most common form and easiest to build. Built using one tall upright that tapers down, via a diagonal rail, to a short upright.

Stile jump: Obstacle based around a footpath access point; usually forms part of a working hunter course, but can be used in the show-jumping arena too.

Trellis wing: Uses the same frame as the pillar or rectangle wing, but with trellis instead of plyboard panels.

Wall: A free-standing filler.

Wing: Part of a show jump that holds jumping poles and rails, sometimes called a stand.

INDEX

Rebecca Skoric